GW00372961

ESSENTIAL PROVENCE AND THE COTE D'AZUR

Original text by Teresa Fisher

Revised and updated by Tristan Rutherford and Kathryn Tomasetti

© AA Media Limited 2011
First published 2008. Content revised and updated 2011

ISBN: 978-0-7495-6794-1

Published by AA Publishing, a trading name of AA Media Limited, whose registered office is Fanum House, Basing View, Basingstoke, Hampshire RG21 4EA. Registered number 06112600.

Colour separation: AA Digital Department
Printed and bound in Italy by Printer Trento S.r.l.

A04193
Maps in this title produced from mapping © MAIRDUMONT/Falk Verlag 2011

About this book

This book is divided into six sections.

The essence of Provence pages 6–19
Introduction; Features; Food and Drink;
Short Break including the 10 Essentials

Planning pages 20–33
Before you go; Getting there; Getting
around; Being there

Best places to see pages 34–55
The unmissable highlights of any visit
to Provence

Best things to do pages 56–73
Best beaches; stunning views; places to
take the children and more

Exploring pages 74–183
The best places to visit in Provence,
organized by area

Maps
All map references are to the maps on
the covers. For example, St-Tropez has
the reference ✚ 19L – indicating the
grid square in which it is to be found

Admission prices
Inexpensive (up to €4);
Moderate (€4 to €8);
Expensive (over €8)

Hotel prices
Price are per room per night:
€ budget (up to €50);
€€ moderate (€50–€100);
€€€ expensive (€100–€200)
€€€€ luxury (over €200)

Restaurant prices
Price for a three-course meal per person
without drinks: € budget (under €25);
€€ moderate (€25–€50);
€€€ expensive (over €50)

Contents

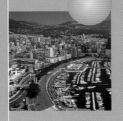

BEST THINGS TO DO

EXPLORING...

The essence of...

The many facets and charms of Provence and the Côte d'Azur lie waiting to be discovered. But with miles of beaches, verdant countryside and Alpine hills, coupled with a jam-packed cultural calendar, it's difficult to know where to start. Should you pack your paintbox, walking boots, swimsuit or skis? Maybe on your first visit concentrate solely on the ambience – the brilliant sunshine, sparkling air, superb food, unforgettable scenery and friendly locals – for it is certain you will become hooked and return again to experience what the addicted already know but keep to themselves!

features

With its exceptional cultural heritage and its rich diversity of landscape, cuisine, climate and peoples, Provence and the Côte d'Azur is France's most visited region. Yet despite its popularity it is still possible to escape the tourist hordes and discover your own hidden delights – tiny sun-kissed vineyards and secret sun-baked coves; bustling markets; romantic châteaux; a dusty game of boules; coffee and croissants in a village cafe; or a glass of pastis in a local bar.

Most visitors to the region are at a loss to know where to start, such is the variety of the landscape and the wealth of ancient history here – but for many, the true essence of Provence can be found in its sleepy medieval villages, precariously perched on steep hillsides or hidden in a landscape of silvery olive groves, vineyards and parasol pines.

The Provençal landscape is splashed with poppy fields and scented stripes of lavender stretching like mauve corduroy across the countryside. It engages your senses: heavy with perfume and painted with the vivid palette of van Gogh and Cézanne.

New visitors soon fall under the region's spell. Those who already know it are enchanted, returning year after year for a taste of *la vie Provençale*.

GEOGRAPHY
- One of 22 regions of France
- *Départements*: Alpes-Maritimes, Alpes-de-Haute-Provence, Bouches-du-Rhône, Hautes-Alpes, Vaucluse and Var
- Surface area: 31,436sq km (12,260sq miles) (Monaco: 2sq km/0.859 mile)
- Protected monuments and buildings: 1,500
- Highest mountain: La Meije (3,983m/13,064ft)

PEOPLE

- Inhabitants: 4.7 million (including 283,500 foreigners); 90% live in large cities and their suburbs
- Largest city: Marseille (population 852,000, or 1.6 million including the city's suburbs)
- Annual visitors to entire region: 35 million
- Annual visitors to coast: over 10 million
- Tourist revenue: €10 billion

AGRICULTURE AND INDUSTRY

- Percentage of France's total production: lemons (70%); cut flowers (50%), fruit and vegetables (20%); rice (25%); melons (30%); olives (52%); grapes (50%)
- Produces 70% of the world's lavender oil
- Flowers produced: 172 million roses; 188 million carnations
- 1,500 fishermen catch 20,000 tonnes (including 10,000 tonnes of sardines)

WINE
- Classified wine regions: 19
- *Appellation d'origine contrôlée* (AOC) wines: 31
- Vineyards: 16 per cent of region's agricultural land; 11 per cent of France's vineyards
- Average size of vineyard: 6ha (15 acres)
- People employed by the wine trade: 20,000

THE ESSENCE OF PROVENCE AND CÔTE D'AZUR

food & drink

France is universally recognized as the world leader in the field of food and wine, and of all its great regional styles *la cuisine Provençale* has one of the strongest personalities; spicy Mediterranean dishes with bold, sun-drenched flavours as varied as its landscapes, leaning heavily on olive oil, tomatoes, garlic and wild herbs. As Peter Mayle justly noted: "Everything is full-blooded. The food is full of strong, earthy flavours ... There is nothing bland about Provence". (*A Year in Provence*)

Provençal specialities include *soupe au pistou* (a springtime vegetable soup, seasoned with garlic and plenty of fresh basil); *beignets de fleurs de courgettes* (courgette flowers dipped in batter and deep fried), *mesclun* (a salad of baby greens, which can include rocket, dandelion and hedge-mustard leaves), *daube* (slow-cooked beef stew with red wine, and citrus zest, *salade Niçoise* (with tuna, egg, black olives and anchovies) and *pain bagnat* (Niçoise salad inside a large bun).

CUISINE NIÇOISE

Within the Provençal tradition, the Nice area has its own distinctive cuisine, reflecting the town's former association with Italy. Pizzas and pastas take on a local flavour, and taste every bit as good in Menton and Nice as they do over the border. Look for *pissaladière* (caramelized onion pizza, eaten as a snack or appetizer), *socca* (thin pancake made of chickpea flour), *petits farcis* (savoury stuffed aubergines, courgettes and tomatoes) and *estocaficada* (stockfish stew).

SURF AND TURF

Near the coast fish dishes reign. Try an authentic bouillabaisse (fish soup), or *bourride*, the poor man's excellent but more economic version. *Moules frîtes* (mussels with french fries) are good value, as are *tellines à la Camarguaise*, tiny clams, sautéed and often served with *aïoli* (garlic mayonnaise). By contrast, meat dishes predominate inland. Try Sisteron lamb with its taste of wild thyme, game dishes, *boeuf*

gardian (a spicy beef stew with olives, served with Camarguais rice) or frogs legs *à la Provençale* (in a butter, parsley and garlic sauce). And don't forget the tasty mountain cheeses, or the lavender-scented honey and truffles.

SWEET THINGS

For those with a sweet tooth there are juicy Cavaillon melons, *pain d'épices* (cinnamon, clove and honey cake), crystallized fruits and candies including burnt-sugar Berlingots from Carpentras and Calissons d'Aix. The village of Sault holds the Guinness record for the world's biggest bag of nougat (3m/10ft high, holding 40,000 pieces).

VIN DE PROVENCE

About 11 per cent of France's wine comes from Provence. The chalky soils and warm, dry Mediterranean climate lend themselves to the development of the smooth, easy-to-drink wines such as Côtes du Ventoux and Côtes du Lubéron. Some of the more famous labels include Côtes du Rhône (➤ 86), notably Gigondas, Vacqueyras and Châteauneuf-du-Pape, a full-bodied,

robust wine with a complex bouquet, perfect with red meats and cheeses.

Provence is particularly famous for its rosé wines, fresh, crisp and fruity, and an ideal accompaniment to seafood. Côtes de Provence and Côteaux d'Aix are numbered among the best. For white wine try the dry, green-tinged Cassis wines (➤ 120) or the fruity Bellet, one of Provence's most original wines and much prized by connoisseurs. Other specialist wines of the region include Listel, a cloudy "grey" rosé and the golden, sultana-flavoured dessert wine, Muscat de Beaumes-de-Venise (➤ 86).

Short break

If you only have a short time to visit Provence and the Côte d'Azur, or would like to get a real flavour of the region, here are some ideas:

● **Soak up the sun on one of the Riviera's sandy beaches,** or relax under the shade of a classic striped parasol (➤ 62–63).

● **Splash through the marshes of the Camargue** on horseback, accompanied by local *gardian* cowboys (➤ 38–39).

● **Taste some of the world's finest wines** at the renowned Châteauneuf-du-Pape (➤ 86–87).

- Spot the rich and famous at the **Cannes Film Festival**, the glitziest, most glamorous event of them all (➤ 24).

- **Join locals in a game of *pétanque* (boules).** This ancient game originated here and, although it is now played all round the world, the most fiercely contested games still take place in the shady squares of Provence. France's largest *pétanque* tournament is held in Marseille's Parc Borély each July.

- **Go shopping in a bright, bustling village market,** and treat yourself to a relaxing picnic of goodies – goat's cheese, tomatoes, olives and wine – in the sleepy surrounding countryside.

- **Taste authentic bouillabaisse** in Marseille, near the old port where the dish originated.

- **Visit a perfumery in Grasse,** and create your very own Provençal scent (▶ 170–171).

● **Try your hand at gambling** in Monte-Carlo's famous casino (➤ 173).

● **Don your diamonds and sparkly** *bijoux* **and stroll along the waterfront at St-Tropez,** admiring the ostentatious yachts and gin palaces (➤ 135).

Planning

Before you go

WHEN TO GO

JAN	FEB	MAR	APR	MAY	JUN	JUL	AUG	SEP	OCT	NOV	DEC
12°C	12°C	14°C	18°C	21°C	27°C	28°C	28°C	25°C	22°C	17°C	14°C
54°F	54°F	57°F	64°F	70°F	81°F	82°F	82°F	77°F	72°F	63°F	57°F

High season   Low season

Temperatures given above are the average daily maximum for each month, although they can rise to 35°C (95°F) in July and August. Spring starts in March when the mimosa and almonds come into bloom on the coast, and it is usually warm enough to sit outside on the terrace in April. Mountain melt-water in spring brings the possibility of flash floods in the Rhône valley. Summers are hot and dry, and the coastal areas are very crowded. There are over 300 days of sunshine a year. The autumn months (September and October) can be very pleasant, although there may be occasional thunderstorms. Colder weather arrives in November, with snow settling on high ground in December. The mistral wind blows down the Rhône valley during the winter months, but you can avoid it by heading east to the Côte d'Azur.

WHAT YOU NEED

● Required   Some countries require a passport to
○ Suggested   remain valid for a minimum period (usually
▲ Not required   at least six months) beyond the date of
entry – check before you travel.

	UK	Germany	USA	Netherlands	Spain
Passport (or National Identity Card where applicable)	●	●	●	●	●
Visa (regulations can change – check before you travel)	▲	▲	▲	▲	▲
Onward or Return Ticket	▲	▲	▲	▲	▲
Health Inoculations (tetanus and polio)	▲	▲	▲	▲	▲
Health Documentation (► 23, Health Insurance)	●	●	▲	●	●
Travel Insurance	○	○	○	○	○
Driving Licence (national)	●	●	●	●	●
Car Insurance Certificate	●	●	●	●	●
Car Registration Document	●	●	●	●	●

WEBSITES

Regional Tourist Organisation,
Provence: www.decouverte-paca.fr

French Tourist Office:
www.franceguide.com

Regional Tourist Organisation, Côte
d'Azur: www.cotedazur-tourisme.com

Monaco Tourist Authority:
www.visitmonaco.com

TOURIST OFFICES AT HOME

In the UK

French Government Tourist Office
Lincoln House
300 High Holborn, WC1V 7JH
☎ 090 68 244 123

Monaco Tourist Office
7 Upper Grosvenor Street
Mayfair, London W1K 2LX
☎ 0207 491 4264

In the USA

French Government Tourist Office
444 Madison Avenue, 16th floor
New York NY10022
☎ 212/838 7800

Monaco Government Tourist Office
565 Fifth Avenue, 23rd floor
New York NY10017 ☎ 212/286 3330

HEALTH INSURANCE

Nationals of EU countries can obtain medical treatment at reduced cost
with the relevant documentation (EHIC – European Health Insurance Card;
www.ehic.org.uk); however this does not apply to Monaco. Private
medical insurance is still advisable for all visitors to France.

Nationals of EU countries can obtain emergency dental treatment at
reduced cost with an EHIC. Around 70 per cent of dentists' standard fees
are refunded. Private medical insurance is still advisable for all.

TIME DIFFERENCES

GMT	France	Germany	USA (NY)	Netherlands	Spain
12 noon	1PM	1PM	7AM	1PM	1PM

France is one hour ahead of Greenwich Mean Time (GMT+1). French
summer time (GMT+2) operates from late March until late October.

NATIONAL HOLIDAYS

1 Jan	*New Year's Day*
27 Jan	*St Devote's Day (Monaco only)*
Mar/Apr	*Easter Sunday and Monday*
1 May	*Labour Day*
8 May	*VE Day (France only)*
May/Jun	*Whit Sunday and Monday*
June	*Corpus Christi (Monaco only)*
14 July	*Bastille Day (France only)*
15 Aug	*Assumption*
1 Nov	*All Saints' Day*
11 Nov	*Remembrance Day (France only)*
19 Nov	*Monaco National Holiday (Monaco only)*
8 Dec	*Immaculate Conception (Monaco only)*
25 Dec	*Christmas Day*

WHAT'S ON WHEN

January *Monte-Carlo Rally* (www.acm.mc)
Monte-Carlo International Circus Festival (www.montecarlofestival.mc)
February *Nice Carnival:* A pre-lenten festival with floats and parades, attracting more than a million spectators to Nice (www.nicecarnaval.com)
Fête du Citron: Floats and displays constructed from tonnes of local citrus produce, Menton (www.feteducitron.com)
Corso fleuri, Bormes-les-Mimosas (www.bormeslesmimosas.com)
March *Monte-Carlo Spring Arts Festival* (www.printempsdesarts.com)
April *Monte-Carlo Tennis Masters Championship*
Wine-growers' Festival, Châteauneuf-du-Pape
Easter Festival and start of bullfighting season, Arles (4 days at Easter)
Fête des Gardians, Arles (www.tourisme.ville-arles.fr)
May *Cannes International Film Festival* (www.festival-cannes.com)
Exporose, Grasse (mid-May, www.ville-grasse.fr)
Fête de la Bravade: Celebrates the town's patron saint, with locals donning traditional costumes and parading St-Torpes's bust through the streets, St-Tropez (16–18 May, ➤ 134)
Formula One Grand Prix, Monaco (www.formula1monaco.com)
Gypsy Pilgrimage, Stes-Maries-de-la-Mer (24–25 May, ➤ 121)

June *Musique dans la Rue:* Jazz, classical and pop concerts held on the streets of Aix-en-Provence (www.aixenmusique.fr)

Sacred Music Festival, Nice: Performances in Nice's Old Town churches (www.opera-nice.org)

Les Fêtes de la Tarasque, Tarascon (last wk of Jun, ➤ 123)

Festival de Marseille: exhibitions, musicals, dance and theatre (through Jul)

July *Nice Jazz Festival:* Held in an olive grove next to the Musée Matisse in Cimiez (3rd wk, www.nicejazzfestival.fr)

Rencontres Internationales de la Photographie, Arles (through Sep)

Festival d'Aix-en-Provence: Opera, dance and theatre (first 3 wks)

Annual Provençal Boules Competition, Marseille (mid-Jul)

Chorègies Music Festival, Orange (last 2 wks, plus first wk of Aug)

Festival d'Avignon: Hugely popular theatre festival known as Festival In

Festival Off: A fringe theatre festival held in Avignon at the same time as its major Festival d'Avignon (www.avignonleoff.com)

International Fireworks Festival, Cannes (www.festival-pyrotechnique-cannes.com)

Corso de la Lavande: Provence's sweetest-smelling festival, celebrating the aromatic lavender plant, Digne-les-Bains (last weekend)

Numerous arts festivals at Arles, Gordes, Fontaine-de-Vaucluse, Menton, Sisteron, St-Paul-de-Vence, Vaison-la Romaine, Vence and other towns and villages (Jul/Aug)

August *Grape-ripening Festival (Fête de la Véraison):* A taste of medieval Provençal life, Châteauneuf-du-Pape (1st weekend)

Monte-Carlo International Fireworks Competition (www.visitmonaco.com)

September *Rice Harvest Festival and end of bullfighting season,* Arles

Les Voiles de St-Tropez Yacht Regatta (end Sep–1st wk Oct)

October *Fiesta des Suds:* International music festival, Marseille

November *Santon Fair,* Marseille (last Sun–Epiphany)

International Dance Festival: Cannes (www.festivaldedanse-cannes.com)

Christmas Mass *Provençal midnight mass* takes place at Aix-en-Provence, Les-Baux-de-Provence, Fontvieille (Monanco), St-Rémy-de-Provence, Séguret, Tarascon and other locations throughout Provence. Check local tourist offices for details.

Getting there

BY AIR

Marseille-Provence Airport		
	🚊	N/A
	🚌	25 minutes
26km (16 miles) to city centre	🚕	30 minutes

Nice-Côte d'Azur Airport		
	🚊	N/A
	🚌	20 minutes
7km (4 miles) to city centre	🚕	15 minutes

The national airline, Air France (☎ 36 54 in France) has scheduled flights from Britain, mainland Europe and beyond, to Marseille and Nice. The airports are also increasingly well-served by low-cost airlines from various UK and European destinations. Nice's airport is Aéroport Nice Côte d'Azur (☎ 08 20 42 33 33 within France; 04 89 88 98 28 from abroad; www.nice.aeroport.fr). Marseille's airport is Aéroport Marseille-Provence (☎ 04 42 14 14 14; www.mrsairport.com).

Either a taxi or the bus will get you to Nice's city centre in about the same time (15-20 minutes), although the taxi is far more expensive. The bus service runs every 20 minutes (6:05am–8:40pm, www. lignedazur.com) from the airport to Nice's *gare routière* (main bus station). Purchase your ticket from the kiosk outside each terminal or from the bus driver. There are also regular buses to Cannes, Monaco and Menton. From Marseille-Provence airport take a taxi to the city or catch a shuttle bus to Marseille St-Charles railway station (25 minutes) or Aix-en-Provence bus station (30 minutes).

EUROTUNNEL

The Eurotunnel shuttle train (☎ 0844 335 3535 within the UK, 08 10 63 03 04 within France;www.eurotunnel.com) takes vehicles and their passengers under the English Channel from Folkestone, in the UK, to Calais/Coquelles, in northern France. The journey takes 35 minutes and is the shortest vehicular journey time from the UK to mainland Europe.

FERRIES

Car ferries link France with the UK. Book early for the cheapest fares.
Brittany Ferries ☎ 0871 244 0744 (within the UK);
www.brittanyferries.com
LD Lines ☎ 0844 576 8836 (within the UK); www.ldlines.com
P&O Ferries ☎ 0871 664 5645 (within the UK); www.poferries.com
Seafrance ☎ 0871 423 7119 (within the UK); www.seafrance.com

BY ROAD

Once in France, a comprehensive system of autoroutes (motorways)
fanning out from Paris enables you to cross the country easily. Your
motoring organisation can recommend a suitable route to your final
destination; or visit www.theAA.com to plan your route online.

BY RAIL

French Railways (SNCF) operate high-speed trains (TGV) directly from
Paris Gare de Lyon to main stations in Provence and the Côte d'Azur. Seat
reservations are required on all TGV trains. For further information contact
SNCF (www.voyages-sncf.com) and Rail Europe (www.raileurope.com).

Getting around

PUBLIC TRANSPORT

Internal Flights Air France (➤ 26) links over 30 cities and towns, among them Marseille, Toulon and Nice.

Trains The main line in Provence and the Côte d'Azur links the towns and cities of the coast with the Rhône valley, with Marseille as its hub. A stretch runs behind the coast from Fréjus/St-Raphaël to Toulon, then along the coast eastwards from Fréjus/St-Raphaël to Menton. In summer this is the most efficient way to get around the region.

Area Buses Services run by a number of private companies are punctual and comfortable, but not very frequent outside main urban areas and coastal resorts. There are also SNCF buses (www.sncf.fr), which serve places on rail routes where trains do not stop. Marseille buses (www.rtm.fr); Nice buses (www.lignedazur.com).

Island Ferries Ferries to the Îles d'Hyères (Porquerolles, Port-Cros and Île de Levant) leave from (Cavalaire, Le Lavandou, Hyêres Port and la Tour-Fondue). Some services operate summer only (www.tlv-tvm.com).

Urban Transport Most sizeable towns have a *gare routière* (bus station), usually near the railway station. Services, even in cities, stop about 9pm.

FARES AND TICKETS

Train tickets can be bought from counters at all SNCF stations and at automatic ticket machines if using a French-issued credit card. Advance bookings can be made online (www.voyages-sncf.com or www.tgv.com).

TGV journeys can be booked up to two months ahead. Contact Rail Europe (☎ 08448 484 064; www.raileurope.co.uk) for information in English about SNCF services.

Discounted tickets are available for children under 12, 12–25 year olds and those over 60.

TAXIS

Taxis are very expensive and not allowed to cruise. They must pick up at ranks *(stations de taxi)* found at airports, railway stations and elsewhere. Always check there is a meter. There is a pick-up charge plus a rate per minute – check with the driver.

DRIVING

- Drive on the right side of the road.
- Seat belts must be worn at all times.
- Random breath-testing is frequent. Never drive under the influence of alcohol.
- Petrol *(essence)*, including unleaded *(sans plomb)* and diesel are widely available. Petrol stations are rarer in mountainous areas. Some on minor roads are closed on Sundays.
- Speed limits on toll motorways: 130kph/81mph (110kph/68mph when wet); non-toll motorways and dual carriageways: 110kph/68mph (100kph/62mph when wet). In fog: 50kph/31mph on all roads.
- A red warning triangle and a high-visibility vest must be carried in your car at all times. Place the triangle 30m (98ft) behind the car in the event of an accident or breakdown. On motorways, ring from emergency phones (every 2km/1 mile) to contact the breakdown service. Off motorways, police will advise on local breakdown services.

CAR RENTAL

All the main car-rental companies have desks at Marseille and Nice airports and in main towns. Car hire is expensive, but airlines and tour operators offer fly-drive packages, and French Railways (SNCF) train-car packages, which are often more economical than hiring locally.

Being there

TOURIST OFFICES
Provence and Côte d'Azur
Comité Régional de Tourisme
Provence-Alpes-Côte d'Azur
Les Docks, 10 place de la Joliette,
13567 Marseille ☎ 04 91 56 47
00; www.decouverte-paca.fr

Départment offices
Comité Régional de Tourisme
Riviéra Côte d'Azur
55 promenade des Anglais, 06000
Nice ☎ 08 92 70 74 07;
www.cotedazur-tourisme.com

Comité Départemental du Tourisme
des Bouches-du-Rhône
Le Montesquieu. 13 rue Roux de
Brignoles, 13006 Marseille ☎ 04 91
13 84 13; www.visitprovence.com

Union Départementale des Offices
de Tourisme et Syndicats d'Initiative
de Vaucluse
12 rue College-de-la-Croix, BP147,
84008 Avignon ☎ 04 90 27 92 76;
www.udotsivaucluse.com

Monaco
Office National du Tourisme de la
Principauté de Monaco
2a boulevard des Moulins
Monte-Carlo, MC 98030 Monaco
☎ 377 92 16 61 16;
www.visitmonaco.com

For tourist offices in other towns
and villages look for 🛈 in the
practical information throughout
the book.

MONEY
The euro is the official currency of France and Monaco. Traveller's cheques
can be used, although major credit cards are much more widely accepted.
Credit and debit cards can be used to withdraw notes from cash machines.

TIPS/GRATUITIES

Yes ✓ No ✗		
Hotels (service included; tip optional)	✗	
Restaurants (service included; tip optional)	✗	
Cafes/bars (service included; tip optional)	✗	
Taxis	✓	€1
Tour guides	✓	€2–5
Porters/ Chambermaids	✓	€1
Toilet attendants	✓	change

POSTAL AND INTERNET SERVICES

The PTT (*Poste et Télécommunications*) deals with mail and telephone services. Letter boxes are yellow. Usual hours are Mon–Fri 8–5, Sat 8–12 (www.laposte.com). Hours may be shorter in rural areas, and post offices may close 12–2. Internet cafes are found in cities, but not often in rural areas. Free wireless internet access is now offered in most hotels.

TELEPHONES

The first two digits of a French telephone number is its area code, which must be included when dialling. The code 377 precedes a number when phoning Monaco from outside the principality.

International dialling codes
To call France: 33, Monaco: 377
From France and Monaco to:
UK: 00 44
Germany: 00 49

USA: 00 1
Netherlands: 00 31
Spain: 00 34
Emergency telephone number
Police: 17 from any call box

EMBASSIES AND CONSULATES

UK
☎ 04 91 15 72 10 (Marseille)
☎ 377 93 50 99 54 (Monaco)
Germany
☎ 04 91 16 75 20 (Marseille)
☎ 04 93 83 55 25 (Nice)
☎ 377 97 77 49 65 (Monaco)
USA
☎ 04 91 54 92 00 (Marseille)

☎ 04 93 88 89 55 (Nice)
Netherlands
☎ 04 91 25 66 64 (Marseille)
☎ 04 93 87 52 94 (Nice)
☎ 377 97 70 36 44 (Monaco)
Spain
☎ 04 91 00 32 70 (Marseille)
377 93 30 24 98 (Monaco)

HEALTH ADVICE

Sun advice Summers, particularly July and August, are dry and hot. If walking, wear a hat and drink plenty of fluids. On the beach, a high-protection sunblock is a must.

Pharmacies Pharmacies (with a green cross sign) have highly qualified staff able to offer medical advice, provide first aid and a wide range of drugs, though some are available by prescription *(ordonnance)* only.

Safe water It is safe to drink tap water served in hotels and restaurants, but never drink from a tap marked *eau non potable*. Bottled water is inexpensive and widely available.

PERSONAL SAFETY

The Police Municipale (blue uniforms) carry police out duties in cities and towns. The Gendarmes (blue trousers, black jackets, white belts) are the national police force and cover the countryside and smaller places. The CRS deal with emergencies and also look after safety on beaches. Monaco has its own police. To avoid danger or theft:

- Do not use unmanned roadside rest areas at night.
- Cars, especially foreign cars, should be secured.

ELECTRICITY

The local power supply is 220 volts and sockets take two-round-pin plugs. British visitors should bring an adaptor and US visitors a voltage transformer.

OPENING HOURS

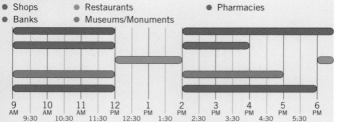

● Shops ● Restaurants ● Pharmacies
● Banks ● Museums/Monuments

In addition to the times shown above, afternoon opening times of shops in summer can be from 4 to 8 or 9pm. Many shops close Sunday–Monday. Small food shops open from 7am and may open Sunday morning. Large department stores do not close for lunch and hypermarkets open 10am to 9 or 10pm but may shut Monday morning. Banks are closed Sunday as well as Saturday or Monday. Museums and monuments have extended summer hours. Many close one day a week; either Monday or Tuesday.

LANGUAGE

French is spoken throughout Provence. In Monaco the traditional Monégasque language (a mixture of French, Provençal and Italian Ligurian) is spoken by the older generation. English is spoken by those involved in tourism and in the larger cosmopolitan centres – less so in smaller, rural places. However, attempts to speak French will always be appreciated. Below is a list of a few helpful words. More extensive coverage can be found in the AA's *French Phrase Book*.

hotel	*l'hôtel*	one/two nights	*une/deux nuits*
room	*la chambre*	reservation	*une réservation*
single room	*une personne*	rate	*le tarif*
double room	*deux personnes*	bathroom	*une salle de bain*
key	*la clé*	toilet	*les toilettes*
bank	*une banque*	banknote	*un billet*
exchange office	*un bureau de change*	change	*la monnaie*
post office	*la poste*	credit card	*une carte de crédit*
foreign exchange	*le change extérieur*	traveller's cheque	*un chèque de voyage*
restaurant	*le restaurant*	lunch	*le déjeuner*
table	*une table*	dinner	*le dîner*
menu	*le menu*	starter	*le hors d'oeuvres*
drink(s)	*une (les) boisson*	main course	*le plat principal*
the bill	*l'addition*	dish of the day	*le plat du jour*
aeroplane	*l'avion*	single/return	*simple/retour*
airport	*l'aéroport*	ticket office	*le guichet*
train station	*la gare*	timetable	*l'horaire*
bus station	*la gare routière*	seat	*une place*
ticket	*un billet*	non smoking	*non-fumeurs*
hello	*bonjour*	thank you	*merci*
goodbye	*au revoir*	sorry	*pardon*
yes	*oui*	excuse me	*excusez-moi*
no	*non*	help!	*au secours!*
please	*s'il vous-plaît*	how much?	*combien?*

Best places to see

1 The Calanques

The most dramatic scenery of the French Riviera – dazzling white cliffs plunging into the sparkling turquoise waters of magnificent mini-fjords.

This fjord-like landscape is unique in Europe. Just outside Cassis, the coast is broken up by a series of tiny, narrow creeks, or *calanques*, lying at the foot of sheer limestone cliffs. The vertical, weathered rock faces are popular with climbers and the clear, deep water is ideal for bathing, making the area a popular weekend retreat from nearby Marseille.

The Calanques can only be reached by pleasure cruiser or kayak from Cassis or on foot, following a waymarked path across the heather and gorse of the high cliff tops, with a steep scramble down to the beaches. The first and longest *calanque*, Port-Miou, is one of the

most picturesque, lined with yachts and pleasure craft. Calanque Port-Pin is the smallest, with a tiny shingle beach shaded by pines (hence the name, although many trees here were destroyed some years ago by a massive forest fire). En Vau, the third inlet, is the most spectacular, with stark precipitous cliffs and needle-like rocks rising from the sea. The 1.5-hour walk to reach it, and the ensuing steep descent to the sandy beach, keeps it free from

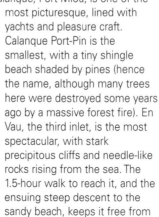

crowds. Or hire a kayak and spend an afternoon exploring En Vau's rocky outcrops.

Further west, the Sormiou and Morgiou creeks can be reached by car. In 1985 French diver Henri Cosquer discovered a Stone Age grotto deep below sea level at Sormiou. It is decorated with ancient paintings of prehistoric animals, similar to those found at Lascaux in the Dordogne, as well as ancient hand tracings. The cave's entrance, at 37m (121ft) below sea level, makes detailed study of paintings both difficult and dangerous.

✚ 13–14L 🖑 Free; boat trips expensive ❓ 45- to 90-minute visits by boat with commentary Feb–Oct daily 9–4; only one trip per day Nov–Jan (www.cassis-calanques.com)
ℹ️ Quai des Moulins, Cassis ☎ 08 92 25 98 92; www.ot-cassis.fr;

2 The Camargue

A strange, disparate marshland, renowned for its passionate people, its traditions, its silver-cream horses, black bulls and salmon-pink flamingos.

No area in France matches the Camargue for its landscape: brackish lagoons, flat rice fields and salty marshes, sand spits and coastal dunes tufted with coarse, spiky grass and interlaced with shallow streams and canals. Even its boundaries, the lesser and greater Rhône deltas and the sea, are forever shifting. This extraordinary landscape harbours an outstanding variety of wildlife and the unique lifestyle of the Camarguais cowboys.

The people of the Camargue are hardy folk. They live in low, thatched, whitewashed cottages with bulls' horns over the door to ward off evil spirits. They proudly guard the Camarguais heritage, by wearing traditional costume and raising horses and cattle on ranches, or *manades*. Contrary to popular belief, the famous white horses are not wild. They are actually owned by a *manadier* or breeder, but are left to roam semi-free. Some are also used for trekking expeditions. The small, black local bulls with their distinctive lyre-shaped horns are bred for the ring. Watching a mounted *gardian* drive his herd through the marshes is a truly unforgettable sight.

The Camargue also offers sanctuary to some of Europe's most exotic water birds, including purple herons and stone curlews. It is the only place in Europe where flamingos breed regularly, reaching their greatest numbers between April and September. The best months for bird watching are from April to June and September to February.

🚩 2E

Parc Ornithologique de Pont-de-Gau (Bird Sanctuary)

✉ DN570 from Arles or Stes-Maries-de-la-Mer ☎ 04 90 97 82 62; www.parcornithologique.com 🕐 Apr–Sep daily 9–dusk; Oct–Mar daily 10–dusk 🖐 Moderate

Manade Jacques Bon, Camargue

✉ Le Mas de Peint, 13200 Le Sambuc ☎ 04 90 97 20 62 ❓ Professional ranch with rodeos and tours on horseback

Musée de la Camargue

✉ Mas du Pont de Rousty ☎ 04 90 97 10 82; www.parc-carmargue.fr 🕐 Apr–Sep Wed–Mon 9-12:30, 1-6; Oct–Dec and Feb–Mar Wed–Mon 10–12:30, 1-5 🖐 Moderate

3 Fondation Maeght, St-Paul-de-Vence

www.fondation-maeght.com

"A world in which modern art can both find its place and that otherworldliness which used to be called supernatural."

These words were spoken by André Malraux, minister of cultural affairs, during the opening of Foundation Maeght in 1964. Since then, this beautiful gallery has become one of the most distinguished modern-art museums in the world. It was the brainchild of Aimé and Marguerite Maeght, who were art dealers and close friends of Matisse, Miró, Braque, Bonnard and Chagall, and it was their private collection that formed the basis of the museum. Their aim was to create an ideal environment in which to display contemporary art, and to achieve this they worked in collaboration with the Catalan architect José-Luis Sert.

The small art gallery that resulted is hidden amid umbrella pines and surrounded by a small park, which contains a collection of sculptures, mosaics and murals. The building itself blends into its natural surroundings, with massive windows, light traps in the roof, and extraordinary white cylindrical "sails" atop the building. These are not solely decorative, but serve the dual purpose of collecting rainwater to work the fountains.

The Fondation Maeght's remarkable permanent collection is comprised entirely of 20th-century art and includes works by nearly every major artist of

the past 60 years. These are shown in rotation throughout the year except during summer when temporary exhibitions are held. The star sights include the Cour Giacometti – a tiled courtyard peopled with skinny Giacometti figures – Chagall's vast, joyful canvas *La Vie*, Miró's *Labyrinthe*, and a fantastic multi-level maze of fountains, trees, mosaics and sculptures.

✚ 22H ✉ St-Paul-de-Vence ☎ 04 93 32 81 63
🕐 Jul–Sep daily 10–7; Oct–Jun daily 10–6 ✋ Expensive
🍴 Cafe (€) ❓ Gift shop, art library

4 Gordes and the Abbaye de Sénanque

www.gordes-village.com

Famous for its artists' colony, magnificent Cistercian abbey and ancient *borie* village, Gordes makes an ideal base for touring the Lubéron.

Gordes is justifiably rated one of the most beautiful villages in France. Its grandiose church and Renaissance **château** rise from a golden plinth on

a spur of Mont Ventoux, surrounded by narrow cobbled streets and tiers of golden sandstone houses that spill down the steep, stony slopes. During World War II many buildings were ruined or abandoned and the village fell into decline until the 1960s, when cubist André l'Hote, constructivist Victor Vasarély and other artists restored the Renaissance houses and set up attractive galleries, studios and boutiques. The château currently contains the **Museum of Pol Mara**, a Flemish contemporary artist and honorary citizen of Gordes.

Southwest of Gordes, the most famous collection of *bories* in France lie hidden in scrubland. These extraordinary beehive-shaped, dry-stone huts sheltered farmers and semi-nomadic shepherds as early as the 3rd century BC, although the bulk of these bories date from between the seventh and 19th centuries. This particular **village** is the largest and most complete of its kind in the world. In a valley north of Gordes is one of the great symbols of Provence, the Cistercian **Abbaye Notre-Dame de Sénanque** – one of France's best remaining examples of 12th-century religious architecture.

➕ 5C
ℹ️ Le Château, Gordes ☎ 04 90 72 02 75
Musée Pol Mara – Château de Gordes
☎ 04 90 72 02 75 🕐 Daily 10–12, 2–6 ✋ Moderate
Village des Bories
✉ D2 from Gordes ☎ 04 90 72 03 48 🕐 Daily 9–dusk
✋ Moderate
Abbaye Notre-Dame de Sénanque
✉ Route de Venasque ☎ 04 90 72 05 72;
www.senanque.fr 🕐 Guided tours daily 10–4 ✋ Moderate

5 Gorges du Verdon

The deepest, longest, wildest canyon in Europe is like a dream come true for sports lovers.

Over the centuries the Verdon river, a tributary of the mighty Durance, has scored an amazing gorge in the limestone plateau of the Alpes-de-Haute-Provence, stretching 21km (13 miles) from the Pont de Soleils to the man-made lake of Ste-Croix. In places it is over 800m (2,624ft) deep, the second deepest gorge in the world after the Grand Canyon and one of Europe's great natural wonders. It was first explored in 1905 by Édouard-Alfred Martel.

The gorge is best approached from Castellane to the east. The bed of the gorge is impassable, and the river is only negotiable by trained sportsmen or with an official guide. Spectacular winding roads hairpin along the clifftops on both sides of the gorge, with frequent *belvédères* to park the car and peer down to the green waters of the Verdon.

Drivers can follow the northern Route des Crêtes, or the southern Corniche Sublime, through the hilltop villages of Trigance and Aiguines. Hardened walkers usually opt for the latter, leaving the road at the Pont Sublime for an awesome eight-hour trek down into the gorge through tunnels and along a series of narrow ledges above the river.

✚ 11C ❓ Walking and climbing: Bureau des Guides de Vardon ☎ 04 92 77 30 50; horseback riding: Ranch Les Pionieers ☎ 04 92 77 38 30; canoeing, rafting, mountain biking: Aqua Viva Est ☎ 04 92 83 75 74
ℹ Verdon Accueil, Aiguines ☎ 04 94 70 21 64; www.aiguines.com

6 Montagne Ste-Victoire

Paul Cézanne was so fascinated by Mont Ste-Victoire that he painted it over 65 times, making this great Provençal landmark famous worldwide.

The Montagne Ste-Victoire lies just east of Aix-en-Provence. Viewed end on, this 16km-long (10 mile) silvery ridge (running east–west) takes the form of a shapely pyramid. On its lower red-soil slopes, Coteaux-d'Aix vineyards give way to dense forest, scrub and fragrant herbs. Above the tree line, the limestone peak reflects every hue in light and shade – blue, grey, white, pink, orange – creating extraordinary designs on the landscape.

For Paul Cézanne, native of Aix, the mountain was a favourite local subject. He painted it again and again from all angles and at all hours, creating some of his greatest canvases including *La Montagne Sainte-Victoire* (1904) and *Le Paysage d'Aix* (1905). In a letter to his son in 1906, he wrote "I spend every day in this landscape, with its beautiful shapes. Indeed, I cannot imagine a more pleasant way or place to pass my time".

Climbing Mont Ste-Victoire requires stout shoes and sure-footedness as, although not the highest mountain in Provence, it is said to be the steepest. It is a steady two-hour hike from les Cabassols on the D10 to the

ruined 17th-century priory and massive Croix de Provence at the 945m (3,100ft) summit. At the eastern base of the mountain is Pourrières wood, where the mountain was named following a Roman victory over invading Germanic tribes.

➕ 15J ❓ The path to the summit may be closed Jul–Sep due to fire risk
ℹ️ 2 place du Général-de-Gaulle, Aix-en-Provence
☎ 04 42 16 11 61; www.aixenprovencetourism.com

7 Musée Matisse, Nice

www.musee-matisse-nice.org

This remarkable collection of Matisse's works, intimate yet instructive and spanning his entire life, is housed in a vivid red villa.

The villa des Arènes is situated on a hill above Nice, at the heart of a 3.6ha (9-acre) olive grove in the district of Cimiez (➤ 161). The villa is an exquisite mid-17th-century folly, with a cleverly painted *tromp l'oeil* facade, colonnaded staircases and terraces are laid out in the Genoese style.

Henri Matisse first came to live in Nice in 1917 and spent long periods of his life near here. Shortly before his death in 1954 he bequeathed his entire personal collection to the city. Together with a second, even larger donation from his wife in 1960 (including over a hundred personal effects from his studio-apartment in the nearby Hotel Regina), it formed the basis of a priceless collection, celebrating the life, work and influence of this great artist. The museum now boasts not only the world's largest collection of Matisse's drawings, but also paintings, photos and a comprehensive selection of his bronze sculptures.

Matisse's entire working life is displayed in the villa, from the old-master copies he made during his apprenticeship period, through an era of sober, dark-toned paintings in the 1890s (including *Intérieur à l'harmonium*), to his Impressionist and fauvist phases (*Jeune femme à l'ombrelle* and *Portrait of Madame Matisse*). The bright colours and simple shapes of his maturity, best portrayed in his decorative paper cut-outs, silk-screen hangings, and works such as *Nu Bleu IV* and *Nature Morte aux Grenades* also feature here.

The large collection of his drawings and engravings (around 450 altogether) are also of interest. The book illustrations for James Joyce's *Ulysses* and the powerful sketches and stained-glass models for the Chapelle du Rosaire at Vence (➤ 177) should definitely not be missed.

🕇 *Nice 4a (off map)* ✉ 164 avenue des Arènes-de-Cimiez
☎ 04 93 81 08 08 🕐 Wed–Mon 10–6 🚌 15, 17, 20, 22, 25
✋ Free; guided tours moderate ❓ Temporary exhibitions

8 Musée Picasso, Antibes

Picasso once had a studio inside this seafront château. Today it houses one of the world's finest collections of his works.

The Grimaldi dynasty ruled for centuries in this beautiful 12th- to 16th-century château, constructed following the design of a Roman fort and occupying a strategic site overlooking the ramparts. In 1928, the city of Antibes acquired the castle to house a museum of art, history and archaeology. When in 1946 Pablo Picasso returned to his beloved Mediterranean, having spent the war years in Paris, he found that he had nowhere suitable to work. The mayor of Antibes lent him a room in Château Grimaldi for use as an atelier and in gratitude Picasso left his entire output of that period on permanent loan to the castle museum, together with a collection of lively ceramics, tapestries and sculptures that he later created in the nearby village of Vallauris: More of his work can be seen in the petite Musée National Picasso La Guerre et La Paix there (www.musee-picasso-vallauris.fr).

Although Picasso spent less than a year in Antibes it was one of his most prolific periods. After the melancholy of war, his work here took on a new

dimension, reflecting the *joie de vivre* of the Mediterranean, bathed in sunny colours and incandescent light. He combined bold new techniques – using industrial paints, fibro-cement and plywood – with ancient themes and mythical images, creating such masterpieces as *Le centaur et le Navire, Ulysee et les Sirènes, Nu couché au lit bleu* and his most famous of all *La Joie de Vivre*.

Most of Picasso's works are exhibited on the two upper floors of the castle. Works by his contemporaries, including Léger, Modigliani and Max Ernst are displayed on the ground floor, along with photographs of the great master at work. On a sunny terrace overlooking the sea, stone and bronze sculptures by Miró, Richier and Pagès are strikingly displayed among cacti, trees and flowers.

✚ 22J ✉ Château Grimaldi, place Mariéjol, Antibes ☎ 04 92 90 54 20 🕐 Mid-Jun to mid-Sep Tue–Sun 10–6; mid-Sep to mid-Jun Tue–Sun 10–12, 2–6 ✋ Moderate

9 Roussillon

It is so easy to fall in love with Roussillon; once known all over the world for its ochre dyes, this beautiful, rosy village glows stop its hilltop perch.

This unforgettable village sits on a platform of rich rust rock called Mont Rouge, surrounded by jagged cliffs and hollows of every shade of ochre imaginable from blood red, gold, orange and pale yellow to white, pink and violet, hidden amid dark pine forests and scrub. For here lie the richest deposits of ochre in all France.

The village of Roussillon was founded by Raymond d'Avignon. According to legend, one day he discovered his wife was having an affair with his page-boy. He killed the page and served his heart

on a platter to his wife. Shocked and distressed, she leapt off the cliffs: her blood formed a spring, permanently colouring the surrounding soil and creating some of the most spectacular scenery in the whole of Provence, from the spiky multi-coloured needles of the "Valley of Fairies" to the brilliantly hued "Cliffs of Blood" and deep gullies of the "Giant's Causeway". Here visitors can explore the old opencast quarries along the 1km (0.5-mile) **Sentier des Ocres** (Ochre Trail), which has information signboards along the way.

The ochre industry began here at the end of the 18th century, bringing prosperity to the villagers until 1958, when competition from cheap synthetic pigments, plus the town's structural instability caused by mining, forced production to stop. Although today very few quarries are worked, Roussillon still holds its merry Journées de l'Ocre (Ochre Festival) at Ascensiontide.

The picturesque houses present a full palette of ochre shades – apricot, pink, violet, gold, mustard, orange, burgundy, russet and brown. The hub of the village is the small, lively square beside the Mairie, where the Roussillonais gather in the outdoor cafes. Narrow lanes and winding stairways lead up to a Romanesque church, offering a sweeping panorama of the ochreous Vaucluse scenery, with its hill villages and distant mountains.

✚ 6C ❓ Ochre festival held in May (Ascension weekend).
ℹ Place de la Poste, Roussillon ☎ 04 90 05 60 25;
www.roussillon-provence.com
Sentier des Ocres
🕐 Daily 9–dusk 🎫 Inexpensive

10 Théâtre Antique, Orange

www.theatre-antique.com

One of the best surviving theatres from the ancient world, built over 2,000 years ago, with seating for up to 10,000 spectators.

The Théâtre Antique was built in the reign of Augustus about AD1, set into the hillside of Colline St-Eutrope at Arausio. Originally there had been a Celtic settlement here, but under Caesar veterans of the second Gallica legion created a major Roman city, building the magnificent theatre, the triumphal arch, temples, baths and many other public buildings.

Although all that remains of the theatre is a mere shadow of its former splendour, it is nevertheless easy to imagine the theatre in its heyday. The cavea, or tiered semicircle, was divided into three levels according to rank. On one tier you can still see the inscription *EQ GIII* meaning "Equus Gradus III" or "third row for horsemen". Senators and guests of honour would occupy marble seats in front of the first row.

The monumental stage wall (*frons scanae*), made from red sandstone and measuring 103m (338ft) long, 37m (121ft) high and nearly 2m (7ft) thick, is the only one in the world to survive completely from ancient times. Louis XIV described it as 'the greatest wall in my kingdom'. Once decorated with 76 columns, friezes, niches and statues, today all the statues have vanished except an imposing marble figure of Emperor Augustus. Beneath the statue is the central "Royal door", and within the wall were

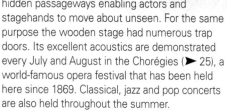

hidden passageways enabling actors and stagehands to move about unseen. For the same purpose the wooden stage had numerous trap doors. Its excellent acoustics are demonstrated every July and August in the Chorégies (➤ 25), a world-famous opera festival that has been held here since 1869. Classical, jazz and pop concerts are also held throughout the summer.

To the west of the theatre, Colline St-Eutrope is well worth the climb to reach its cool, shady park with magnificent views over Orange, the theatre and the Rhône plain beyond.

✚ 3A ✉ Rue Madeleine Roch ☎ 04 90 51 17 60
🕐 Jun–Aug daily 9–7; Jan, Feb, Nov, Dec daily 9:30–4:30; Mar, Oct daily 9:30–5:30; Apr, May, Sep daily 9–6
✋ Moderate, includes audio-guide and is also valid for Musée Municipal ❓ Telephone for details of guided tours for groups, concert and theatre information

Best things to do

Best things to buy

Antiques: Second-hand and antique stores cover the entire region. The best antiques markets are in Nice and L'Isle-sur-la-Sorgue.

Ceramics – Vallauris and Moustiers-Sainte-Marie: Provence's two ceramic centres focus on sculpture and delicate faïence respectively.

Linen: Visitors will spot Provençal table spreads and hand-spun cloth in every town.

Olive Oil – Alpes-Maritimes: Find bottles of bright green local oil in green grocers, wine shops and markets all over the region.

Rice – Camargue: This short, sticky rice from the Camargue wetlands makes a great gift.

Santons – Bouches-de-Rhône: Translated as "little saints", santons are charming model figures representing everyday characters in Provençal life.

Soap – Marseille: Vegetable oil soap has been made in Marseille for centuries. Traditional square blocks, and more contemporary flavoured soaps, are available all over Provence.

Wine – coastal Provence: Provence's wine industry basks in mild winters and sunny summers. The best appellations are Côte du Provence, Bandol and Bellet.

Outdoor activities

Take a helicopter from Nice Airport to Monte-Carlo or book a sight-seeing flight.
Héli Air Monaco ☎ 04 93 21 34 95; www.heliairmonaco.com

Rent a speedboat, and putter around the Côte d'Azur.
Dark Pelican ☎ 04 93 01 76 54; www.darkpelican.com

Visit the Îles de Lérins, the deserted islands of the coast, by taking a 15-minute boat ride from Cannes or Juan-les-Pins.
Trans Cote d'Azur ☎ 04 92 98 71 30; www.trans-cote-azur.com

Hang-glide in Haute-Provence
Ecole de Parapente ☎ 04 75 28 51 39; www.provence-parapente.com

Take a boat trip to Corsica from Nice's old port.
Corsica Ferries ☎ 04 95 32 95 95; www.corsicaferries.com

Ski Serre-Chevalier, Provence's largest ski resort.
☎ 04 92 24 98 98; www.serre-chevalier.com

Hire a Harley Davidson and cruise the streets of St-Tropez.
Espace 83 ☎ 04 94 55 80 00

Take the "Pinecone Train" along the scenic route from Nice to Digne-les-Bains (➤ 144).
☎ 04 97 03 80 80; www.trainprovence.com

Kayak or canoe through the beautiful Gorges du Verdon.
Aqua Viva Est ☎ 04 92 83 75 74; www.aquavivaest.com

Go horseback riding in the Massif de l'Esterel or the Massif
des Maures.
César et Léonie ☎ 04 94 45 11 43; www.cesar-et-leonie.com

Best beaches

Calanques, Cassis: Turquoise water and white sandy beaches.
✛ 14L

Cannes: The best beaches in the region for star-spotting.
✛ 21J

Esterel Massif: Tiny sandy coves dotted along this wild and unspoilt stretch of coast to the east of Le Trayas.
✛ 20–21K

Fréjus-Plage: Best for families; plenty of water sports on offer.
✛ 20K

Juan-les-Pins: The first summer resort on the Riviera.
 22J

Menton: This attractive Italianate town with its many semi-tropical gardens, boasts the best sunshine record in France.
✚ 24H

Plage de la Briande, St-Tropez: The most deserted St-Tropez beach, with fine golden sand.
✚ 19M

Plage de la Garoupe, Cap d'Antibes: A good beach for children; safe, shallow water and interesting rocks to explore.
✚ 22J

Plage de la Palud, Port-Cros, Îles d'Hyères: Best island beach.
✚ 18M

La Voile Rouge, St-Tropez: The trendiest and most frivolous of the beach strips on the Baie de Pampelonne.
✚ 20L

Top markets

Aix-en-Provence
Aix's flower market encapsulates the fragrances and colours of Provence.
✉ Place d'hôtel de Ville 🕓 Tue, Thu, Sat am

Arles
An opportunity to see the Arlésienne women in traditional dress. Fruit, vegetables, soaps and fabrics, also saddles and stirrups.
✉ Boulevard des Lices 🕓 Sat am

Avignon
One of the region's best Christmas markets is held here, with dozens of small wooden chalets selling arts, crafts, decorations, truffles, nougats, wines and regional specialities.
✉ Place de l'Horloge 🕓 Dec

Carpentras
A truffle market draws gourmet chefs and shoppers alike from all over France.
✉ Allée des Platanes 🕓 Nov–Mar Fri am

Cavaillon
A great fresh produce market.
✉ Place du Cros 🕓 Mon am

Isle-de-la-Sorgue

A flea market that lines the quays of the pea-green river Sorgue is the largest outside Paris, selling everything from bric-à-brac and antiquities to fine wine, cheese and olive oils.

✉ Quai de la Gare and Village des Antiquaires ⏰ Sun

Marseille

Fascinating secondhand and rare book market.

✉ Cours Julien ⏰ Every 2nd Sat of month

Fresh fish market with ad hoc harbourside stalls.

✉ Quai des Belges ⏰ Daily

Nice

Voted one of France's most exceptional markets, with fresh fruit, vegetables, flowers and local specialities such as *socca*. The same street also hosts an antiques market.

✉ Cours Saleya ⏰ Tue–Sun; antiques Mon

St-Tropez

One of the region's largest markets with colourful stalls of mouth-watering local delicacies, antiques, fashions, fabrics, arts and crafts.

✉ Place des Lices ⏰ Tue and Sat

Stunning views

From the summit of Mont Vinaigre in the Massif de l'Esterel (➤ 140–141).

From the Exotic Gardens in Èze, across to Corsica (➤ 170).

Frequent viewpoints along the Corniche Moyenne (➤ 169).

The richly coloured ochre cliffs of Roussillon at sunset (➤ 52–53).

From the D53 road looking down over Monaco (➤ 172).

From Colline du Château, the headland at the end of the promenade des Anglais, Nice (➤ 160).

From the ruined 11th-century chateau above Grimaud (➤ 142).

From the Pic du Cap Roux, the highest point of the Corniche de l'Esterel (➤ 140–141).

Along the Route des Crêtes in the Gorges du Verdon (➤ 44–45).

Hilltop villages

Bormes-les-Mimosas: A flower-filled village and regional gourmet capital (➤ 138–139).

Entrevaux: Medieval outpost, towering above a gorge in the Var river (➤ 144–145).

Èze: Glamorous, arty and a touch touristy, but with great views over the Riviera (➤ 170).

Gordes: The Lubéron's prettiest village is like a film-set backdrop (➤ 42–43).

Grimaud: Spend hours wandering the castle and winding streets (➤ 142.)

Moustiers-Ste-Marie: Find ceramics, linens and fine dining in this gateway to the Gorges du Verdon (➤ 44–45).

Saorge: Italiante hilltown tumbling down the Roya valley (➤ 175).

St-Paul-de-Vence: A must for art-lovers, and an ex-haven for scores of contemporary artists (➤ 176).

Great gardens

Château d'Entrecasteaux Gardens

Designed by Le Nôtre, creator of the gardens of the Palais de Versailles.

🔢 17J ✉ Entrecasteaux ☎ 04 94 04 43 95; www.chateau-entrecasteaux.com 🕐 Easter–Oct Mon–Fri during daylight hours

Domaine du Rayol

Seaside botanical gardens with an underwater snorkelling trail, plus Amazonian and Mediterranean gardens.

🔢 18M ✉ Avenue des Belges, Rayol-Canadel ☎ 04 98 04 44 00; www.domainedurayol.org 🕐 Jul, Aug 9:30–7:30; Apr–Jun, Sep, Oct 9:30–6:30; Nov–Jan 9:30–5:30

Fondation Maeght

The gardens of Fondation Maeght feature sculptures by Miró, a courtyard peopled by Giocometti figures and a small chapel with a stained-glass window by Braque.

🔢 22H ✉ 623 chemin de Gardettes, St-Paul de Vence ☎ 04 93 32 81 63; www.fondation-maeght.com 🕐 Jul–Sep 10–6

Jardin Exotique, Èze

Over 400 cacti and succulents surrounding the ruins of the castle, with great views.

🔢 23H ✉ Èze village ☎ 04 93 41 10 30 🕐 During daylight hours

Jardin Exotique, Monaco

Six thousand cacti and

succulents tumble down the cliff edge high above Monaco-ville.
✚ 23H ✉ 62 boulevard du Jardin Exotique, Monaco ☎ 04 93 41 10 30;
www.jardin-exotique.mc ◉ Jan to mid-Nov 9–6

Jardin Val Rameh

A tropical garden with giant lilly pads, rainforest trees and roses.
✚ 24H ✉ Avenue St Jacques, Menton ☎ 04 93 35 86 72; www.jardins-
menton.fr ◉ Arp–Sep 10–12:30, 3:30–6:30; Oct–Mar Wed–Mon 10–12:30,
2–5

Phoenix Parc Floral

The vast 22m high (72ft) glass-and-metal "Green Diamond"
counts among the world's largest greenhouses.
✚ 22H ✉ 405 Promendade des Anglais, Nice ☎ 04 92 29 77 00 ◉ Year
round 9:30–dusk

Renoir's Garden

Wild, unkept piece of land dotted with gnarled 1,000-year-old
olive trees.
✚ 22H ✉ Chemin des Collettes, Cagnes-sur-Mer ☎ 04 93 20 61 07
◉ Jun–Aug Wed–Mon 10–12, 2–6; Sep–May Wed–Mon 10–12, 2–5

Villa Ephrussi de Rothschild

Ornamental gardens including Florentine, Japanese, exotic and
rose gardens.
✚ 23H ✉ Saint Jean Cap Ferrat ☎ 04 93 01 33 09; www.villa-
ephrussi.com ◉ Year round 10–dusk

Villa Kérylos

Olive trees, vines, oleanders, papyrus, pomegranate, carob and
other typically Greek plants.
✚ 23H ✉ Impasse Gustave Eiffel, Beaulieu-sur-Mer ☎ 04 93 01 01 44;
www.villa-kerylos.com ◉ Jul–Aug 10–7; mid-Feb to Jun, Sep, Oct 10–6;
Nov to mid-Feb Sat, Sun 10–6, Mon–Fri 2–6

Places to take the children

Antibes Land
All ages enjoy this amusement park.

✉ Route N7, Antibes ☎ 04 93 33 41 43; www.azurpark.com ◐ Early Jul–Aug daily 5pm–2am; mid-Jun to early Jul Mon–Fri 8:30pm–1am, Sat–Sun 4pm–1am; Sep Sat–Sun 4pm–2am; Apr to mid-Jun Sat–Sun 2–7pm

Aquacity
Splash away countless hours in this aquatic paradise.

✉ 13240 Septemes-les-Vallons (off Aix–Marseille autoroute), Marseille ☎ 04 91 51 54 08; www.aquacity.fr ◐ Mid-Jun to Aug daily 10–7; Jun–early Sep daily 10–6

Aqualand
This fantastic waterpark appeals to all the family.

✉ Quartier le Capou, Fréjus, RN98 ☎ 04 94 51 82 51; www.aqualand.fr ◐ Jul–Aug daily 10–7; Jun, Sep daily 10–6

Azur Park
Nearly 30 child-friendly rides, from slides to water bumper cars.

✉ Gassin, Golfe de St-Tropez ☎ 04 98 12 62 90; www.azurpark.com ◐ Jun–Aug 8pm–1am; May, Sep 7pm–midnight; Apr 4pm–midnight

Magic Parkland
Pony rides, wild west shows and fairground rides.

✉ 13820 Ensuès la Redonne ☎ 04 42 79 86 90; www.magic-park-land.com ◐ Jul–Aug daily 10–6; Mar–Jun, Sep Sat–Sun 10-6; Oct Sun 10–6

Marineland

A wonderful world of performing sea lions, killer whales and dolphins. Exotic butterflies, face painting, water slides and crazy-golf.

✉ Route N7 (opposite Antibes Land), Antibes ☎ 04 93 33 49 49; www.marineland.fr ⏰ Jul–Aug daily 10–11; Apr–Jun, Sep daily 10–7; Feb–Mar daily 10–6

Musée Oceanographique de Monaco

Jars of spooky sea life, a blue whale skeleton and artefacts from several polar missions will appeal to all ages.

✉ Avenue Saint-Martin, Monaco ☎ 0377 93 15 36 00; www.oceano.org ⏰ Jul–Aug 9:30–7:30; Apr–Jun, Sep 9:30–6:30; Oct–Mar 10–6

Parc Zoologique la Barben

Children love this modern zoo, with spacious enclosures for elephants, giraffes, tigers and white rhinos. Picnic area and playground, too.

✉ Route D572, between Salon-de-Provence and Aix-en-Provence ☎ 04 90 55 19 12; www.zoolabarnen.com ⏰ Daily 10–6 (Jul–Aug until 7)

Tiki III

See the bulls, horses and wild birds of the Camargue on a 90-minute mini cruise by a paddle boat.

✉ D38, 1.5km (0.75 mile) from Stes-Maries-de-la-Mer ☎ 04 90 97 81 68; www.tiki3.fr ⏰ Mid-Mar to mid-Nov, multiple departures daily, telephone to confirm times

Visiobulle

Discover the underwater world of "Millionaire's Bay" in a glass-bottomed boat. Advance booking recommended.

✉ Embarcadère Courbet, Juan-les-Pins ☎ 04 93 67 02 11; www.visiobulle.com ⏰ Jul–Aug 9:25, 10:40, 11:55, 2, 3:25, 4:50, 6:15; Apr–Jun, Sep daily 11, 1:30, 3, 4:30

Exploring

Provence and the Côte d'Azur together form the world's most sophisticated holiday playground, thanks mainly to their exceptional cultural heritage and their rich diversity of landscapes. The very name Côte d'Azur conjures up images of lazy days, sunny blue skies, glittering seas and sandy beaches. With such chic, see-and-be-seen resorts as Nice, Monaco and St-Tropez, it is easy to be seduced by the charms of the coast. But venture inland, and you will find enchanting red-roofed farmsteads hidden amidst vineyards and lavender-striped fields; wild alpine scenery fragrant with the perfumes of Provence; and beautiful sun-drenched villages. Add brilliant sunshine and the *joie de vivre* of a Mediterranean lifestyle, and it is little wonder Provence is France's most visited region.

Avignon and Vaucluse

Avignon

Despite being one of France's smallest *départements*, the Vaucluse has been blessed with more than its fair share of beautiful scenery and treasures. A region of colourful, bustling markets, swift-flowing rivers, sweetly scented *garrigue*, brilliant red and yellow ochre cliffs, and world-famous wines. The timeless quality of its sun-bleached landscapes is reinforced by some of the finest Roman remains, at Orange and Vaison-la-Romaine, and the entire region is saturated in medieval buildings, from the remotest hilltop village to the papal grandeur of Avignon.

For many, the Lubéron region epitomizes the real magic of Provence – timeless villages dozing under blue skies, ornamental fountains splashing in the sleepy squares and villagers playing boules under shady plane trees or enjoying a simple meal while gazing out over silvery olive groves, scented fig trees and neat rows of lavender.

AVIGNON

The city of Avignon – administrative centre of the Vaucluse and a major artistic hub – is one of the most important cities in the history of France. Strategically located near the junction of the Rhône and Durance rivers, it has been the scene of countless conflicts since Roman times, and for over a century it was the seat of the popes and centre of a religious and political power struggle.

It was a French pope, Clement V, who first moved his residence from the Vatican to Avignon in 1309. For the next seven decades, a succession of French popes and cardinals built up a powerful base here, constructing a cornucopia of architectural treasures within the city's fortifications to display their wealth and power. Following pressure from the rest of Europe, the papal establishment finally transferred back to Rome in 1377. But a group of French cardinals refused to accept this and elected a series of rival antipopes who, over the next 40 years, continued to exercise authority from Avignon, creating what is today known as the Great Schism.

A walk along the ramparts reveals the two sides of Avignon today – the village-like atmosphere of the historic walled old town, its skyline adorned with steeples and monuments, and the sprawling factories and bustling modern suburbs beyond, accommodating the city's 100,000 inhabitants. It is a lively tourist centre, especially in July when the narrow lanes and pedestrian zones resound with buskers, street theatre and cafe cabarets.

www.ot-avignon.fr

✚ 4C

🛈 41 cours Jean-Jaurés, Avignon ☎ 04 32 74 32 74

Collection Lambert

Avignon's only international contemporary art museum opened in 2000. Set around a leafy courtyard, the Collection Lambert organises three large-scale temporary exhibitions each year.
www.collectionlambert.com

✉ 5 rue Violette ☎ 04 90 16 56 20 🕐 Jul, Aug 11–7; Sep–Jun Tue–Sun 11–6 ✋ Moderate ❓ Cafe, giftshop

Musée Angladon

This museum, located in an elegant city mansion, houses the prestigious collection of former residents Jean and Paulette Angladon-Dubrujeaud, including paintings by Sisley, Manet, Cézanne and Picasso, as well as Provence's only original van Gogh.

www.angladon.com

✉ 5 rue du Laboureur ☎ 04 90 82 29 03 🕓 Mid-Apr to mid-Oct Tue–Sun 1–6; mid-Oct to mid-Apr Wed–Sun 1–6 ✋ Moderate

Musée Calvet

The private art collection of physician Dr Esprit Calvet (1728–1810) provides a comprehensive study of the French and Avignon schools of painting and sculpture from the 15th to 20th centuries, including works by Jacques-Louis David, Modigliani and Manet.

www.musee-calvet.org

✉ 65 rue Joseph Vernet ☎ 04 90 86 33 84 🕓 Wed–Mon 10–1, 2–6 (7 in summer) ✋ Moderate

Place de l'Horloge

A lively square, abuzz with cafes, artists and buskers. Site of Avignon's Christmas markets (➤ 65).

Palais des Papes

The majestic, monumental Pope's Palace was built in a spacious cobbled square as a symbol of the papal residency in Avignon. Its massive walls shelter a labyrinth of halls, courtyards and chambers divided into the Old Palace, built by Pope Benedict XII between 1334 and 1342, and the New Palace, begun under his successor, Pope Clement VI and completed in 1348. Each part has its own

distinctive character. Benedict XII's Old Palace has an almost austere, monastic simplicity in stark contrast with the New Palace.

Clement VI was an ardent patron of the arts, displaying his wealth and power in lavish frescoes and flamboyant ceilings. His ostentatious New Palace received a mixed reception. Medieval chronicler Froissart pronounced it "the finest and strongest palace in the world" whereas Petrach called it "Unholy Babylon … a sewer where all the filth of the universe has gathered". The entire complex is so vast that it has been described as "a city within a city" and takes at least half a day to visit if you're keen to see it all. Don't miss the fanciful Audience Hall, the frescoes of the Stag Room, the papal bedroom, St Martial's Chapel and the Hall of the Consistory.
www.palais-des-papes.com

✉ Place du Palais des Papes ☎ 04 90 27 50 00 🕓 Jul to mid-Sep daily 9–8 (Aug 9–9); Mar–Jun, mid-Sep to Nov 9–7; Dec–Feb 9:30–5:45 🍴 Cafe (€) ✋ Expensive

Petit Palais

The beautifully restored former residence of the bishops of
Avignon was converted in 1958 to house two important collections
– medieval works from the Musée Calvet and the Campana
collection of 13th- to 16th-century Italian paintings from the
Louvre. The medieval works include 600 sculptures and around 60
paintings, such Sandro Botticelli's *Madonna and Child*.

www.petit-palais.org

✉ Palais des Archevèques, place du Palais des Papes ☎ 04 90 86 44 58
🕐 Wed–Mon 10–1, 2–6 💵 Moderate

Pont St-Bénézet

This famous bridge, immortalized in the popular 16th-century song *Sur le pont d'Avignon*, was one of the first bridges built across the Rhône. Originally made of wood, it was reconstructed in stone at the end of the 13th century. Only four of its 22 arches remain, together with the tiny chapel of St Nicholas on the second pier. The song about dancing on the bridge is famous worldwide, but it was actually under the arches of the bridge *(sous le pont)*, on the Île de la Barthelasse, that the people of Avignon used to dance.

✉ Rue Ferruce ☎ 04 90 27 51 16 🕓 Jul to mid-Sep daily 9–8 (Aug 9–9); mid-Mar to Jul, mid-Sep to Nov 9–7; Dec to mid-Mar 9:30–5:45 ✋ Moderate

Vaucluse

CARPENTRAS

This prosperous market town, beside the Auzon river and at the heart of the Côtes du Ventoux wine region, was the old capital of Venasque (then called the Comtat Venaissin) from the 14th century until the Revolution. During its Friday morning market the shady plane-tree lined avenues of the old town are filled with the colours and fragrances of Provence alongside Carpentras's specialities – truffles, candied fruits and the stripey sweets called *berlingots*.

In the heart of town a small triumphal arch with vivid carvings of chained prisoners marks the Roman period at Carpentras, whereas the nearby Porte d'Orange is the only surviving part of the medieval ramparts. Other notable buildings include the Gothic **Cathédrale St-Siffrein** and France's oldest **synagogue,** which dates back to 1327.

www.carpentras-ventoux.com

✚ 5B

ℹ 97 place du 25 Août 1944, Carpentras ☎ 04 90 63 00 78

Cathédrale St-Siffrein

✉ Place Générale-de-Gaulle ☎ 04 90 63 08 33 🕐 Daily 7:30–12, 2–6:30

Synagogue

✉ Place Maurice Charretier ☎ 04 90 63 39 97 🕐 Mon–Thu 10–12, 3–5, Fri 10–12, 3–4. Closed Sat, Sun, public hols and Jewish hols 🎟 Free

CAVAILLON

Cavaillon is France's greatest market garden – its very name synonymous with delicious, sweet, pink-fleshed melons – and

holds one of Europe's largest wholesale fruit and vegetable markets. The mouth-watering market every Monday morning is considered the most important in the Vaucluse.

The town's agricultural wealth stems from its location in the fertile Durance valley. From the Colline St-Jacques, a one-time neolithic site at the top of the town, there are spectacular views across the valley to the distant highlands of the Lubéron and the Alpilles. Back in the town centre, Roman finds have been assembled in the Musée Archéologique. The former cathedral is also worth visiting, as is the beautifully preserved 18th-century synagogue, with its small museum illustrating the region's traditional protection of Jewish communities.

www.cavaillon-luberon.com

➕ 5C

ℹ Place François-Tourel, Cavaillon ☎ 04 90 71 32 01

CÔTES DU RHÔNE VILLAGES

The stony, sun-baked red-clay soil of the southern Rhône nurtures some of France's most prestigious wines of which the best known is Châteauneuf-du-Pape. Numerous wine routes lead you through charming villages hidden in a sea of vineyards. Restaurants and wine cellars en route offer wine-tastings.

Beaumes-de-Venise

Majestically framed by the lacy silver crags of the Dentelles de Montmirail, Beaumes is well-known for its sweet golden Muscat wines. Taste them at the Cave des Vignerons or during the region's annual wine festivals accompanied by goats' cheeses, *foie gras* and melons drowned in Muscat.

www.ot-beaumesdevenise.com

➕ 5A

ℹ️ Place du Marché, Beaumes-de-Venise ☎ 04 90 62 94 39

Châteauneuf-du-Pape

The wines of Châteauneuf-du-Pape are world-renowned, largely thanks to 14th-century Pope Jean XXII of Avignon. It was he who built the now-ruined château, with its splendid views, as a summer residence and planted the first vineyards. Many Côtes du Rhône wines are made from just one grape variety, but vintners here blend up to 13 different grapes to produce their distinctive wines of unique complexity. The Musée du Vin Père Anselme here is dedicated to the history of

local viticulture and visitors can indulge in wine tastings.
www.ccpro.it

✚ 4B ❓ Wine festivals in Apr and Aug (➤ 24, 25).

ℹ Place du Portail,
Châteauneuf-du-Pape

☎ 04 90 83 71 08

Gigondas

The wines of this small,
unspoiled village, set
against the jagged
backdrop of the
Dentelles, are reputed to
be the best in the area.
www.gigondas-dm.fr

✚ 4A

ℹ Rue du Portail, Gigondas

☎ 04 90 65 85 46

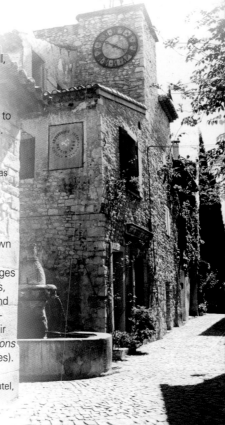

Séguret

This charming circular
hilltop village has its own
*appellation d'origine
contrôlée*. Ochre cottages
with turquoise shutters,
hidden behind vines and
creepers, house crafts-
men renowned for their
dried flowers and *santons*
(Christmas crib figurines).

✚ 5A

ℹ Place du Chanoine-Sautel,
Vaison-la-Romaine

☎ 04 90 36 02 11

FONTAINE-DE-VAUCLUSE

Tucked away at the end of the narrow *vallis clausa* (enclosed valley), after which the whole Vaucluse *département* is named, Fontaine-de-Vaucluse is famous for its emerald-green spring, which gushes from a huge cave-like abyss at the foot of a 230m (754ft) cliff. Research has proved that this is one of the world's largest and most powerful springs. It consists of a vast underground labyrinth of rivers covering over 2,000sq km (780sq miles) and is able to produce up to 200,000 litres (44,000 gallons) of water per second at certain times of year. Pagan Gauls believed it to be the home of a god, while Christians named it the Devil's Hole. Fontaine's other attractions include a small **museum** dedicated to the 14th-century Italian poet Petrarch. He wrote most of his poetry during a 16-year stay here, inspired by the solitude and wilderness.

www.oti-delasorgue.fr

➕ 5C

ℹ Résidence Jean Garcin, Fontaine-de-Vaucluse ☎ 04 90 20 32 22

Moulin à Paper Vallis Clausa

✉ Chemin du Gouffre ☎ 04 90 20 34 14 🕐 Jul–Aug daily 9–12:15, 2–7; Sep–Jun daily 9–12:15, 2–6 🎫 Free

Musée-Bibliothèque François Pétrarque

✉ Rive gauche de la Sorgue ☎ 04 90 20 37 20 🕐 Jun–Sep Wed–Mon 10–12:30, 1:30–6; Apr–May, 1–15 Oct Wed–Mon 10–12, 2–6 🎫 Inexpensive

THE LUBÉRON

The **Parc Naturel Régional du Lubéron** is a protected region of cedar and pine countryside interspersed with lavender fields, almond and olive groves, fragrant herbs, *garrigue* scrub and vineyards, draped across a compact range of small mountains that stretch from Cavaillon to Manosque.

The dramatic wooded gorge of the Combe de Lourmarin (road D943) splits the region in two. The high, wild Grand Lubéron mountains lie to the east. The climb from Auribeau to the uppermost peak of Mourre Nègre (1,100m/3,608ft) affords views from the Basse-Alpes to the Mediterranean. To the west, the pretty hilltop villages of the Petit Lubéron have long been one of France's most fashionable *residences secondaires*.

✠ 6C

Parc Naturel Régional du Lubéron

🛈 Maison du Parc, place Jean-Jaurès, Apt

☎ 04 90 04 42 00; www.parcduluberon.fr

🕐 Mon–Fri 8:30–12, 1:30–6

Apt

This busy old market town north of the Lubéron mountains makes an ideal base for touring the area. The best place to start is at the Maison du Parc Naturel Régional du Lubéron, which details walks and other outdoor activities, together with a small museum documenting local natural history.

The town itself is surrounded by fruit trees and is renowned for its jams. Apt is also well known for its lavender essence and handmade pottery and is an important centre for the truffle trade in winter.

www.ot-apt.fr

✠ 6C

🛈 20 avenue Philippe-de-Girard, Apt ☎ 04 90 74 03 18

Bonnieux

The terracotta-roofed houses of
Bonnieux wind up to a tiny 12th-
century chapel surrounded by
sentinel-like cypresses. The
village is spread out on a north-
facing spur of the Petit Lubéron
overlooking the vineyards, cherry
trees and lavender fields of the
Coulon valley, and its *belvédère*
commands entrancing views
over the Plateau de Vaucluse to
mighty Mont Ventoux beyond. Once papal property, Bonnieux has
preserved many fine monuments including the Town Hall, a bakery
museum and some Renaissance paintings in its two churches.

✚ 6C

🛈 7 place Carnot, Bonnieux ☎ 04 90 75 91 90

Gordes

Best places to see, ➤ 42–43.

Lourmarin

A Renaissance château, medieval houses made from yellow stone
and dressed in honeysuckle, tiny fountain-filled squares and many
inviting restaurants create a pretty ensemble on the southern
slopes of the Lubéron. French novelist and philosopher Albert

Camus bought a house here
after winning the Nobel Prize
for literature in 1957. His grave
is in the village cemetery.

www.lourmarin.com

✚ 6D

🛈 9 avenue Philippe-de-Girard,
Lourmarin ☎ 04 90 68 10 77

Ménerbes

The Luberón's highest-profile village has long attracted celebrities, including Picasso's mistress Dora Maar, François Mitterand and Peter Mayle. Sadly, this scenic, once off-the-beaten-track village, perched high above neat rows of vines, has suffered from its association with Mayle (who lived in a *mas* near by until he was driven away by hoards of visiting fans!). But it remains a lively village with a dynamic weekly market, 13th-century fortress and 14th-century church.

✚ 5C

🛈 Bonnieux Tourist Office (➤ opposite)

Oppède-le-Vieux

At first glimpse Oppède appears to be a typical Provençal village of narrow streets, stairways and attractive cream-coloured houses tumbling down the hillside, all crowned by an impressive ruined château. On closer inspection you will see that many of the houses are gutted ruins, overrun with weeds. The village was abandoned in the late 19th century, following the tyrannical reign of Baron Oppède who sold over 800 villagers as slaves in Marseille. In recent years, the Romanesque church and some of the old quaint cottages have been restored by residents and Oppède is returning to its former glory.

✚ 5C

a drive around the Lubéron

Starting in Apt, take the D22 northeast towards Rustrel, then right at the crossroads to Bouvene.

The enormous old ochre quarries of Colorado de Rustrel are a colourful tourist attraction – an almost lunar landscape of mounds, pillars, cliffs and hollows in every imaginable shade of ochre from pale yellow to blood red, set against deep pine forest. (From Bouvene it is a 50-minute walk.)

Back at the crossroads, continue straight (heading northeast) on along the D179 then the D943 to St-Saturnin-lès-Apt. Leave the village on the D2 to Gordes (➤ 42–43). After Gordes, continue along the D2 towards Cavaillon, then take the first left (D103) signposted Apt and Beaumettes. Go straight on at the roundabout, following signs up to the centre of Ménerbes (➤ 91).

Outside Ménerbes, the Domaine de la Citadelle has a museum of corkscrews (Musée du Tire-Bouchon) dating back to the 17th century, with complimentary wine tasting.

Leave Ménerbes on the D103 then bear left on the D109 past the Renaissance abbey of St-Hilaire to Lacoste.

Lacoste vies with neighbouring villages Ménerbes, Bonnieux and Oppède for the title of prettiest Lubéron village – a cinematic hilltop village, rich, exclusive and crowned by an 11th-century fortress, which in its heyday was one of the region's grandest. Today the fortress is owned by renowned fashion designer Pierre Cardin.

*Further along the D109 you reach Bonnieux (➤ 90).
Leave the village heading northeast on the D3, then turn
first left (D149) to Pont Julien.*

This bridge is reputedly the best-preserved Roman bridge
in France.

*Turn right at the main road (N100) for the return journey
to Apt.*

Distance 90km (56 miles)
Time 2.5 hours without stops; full day with visits
Start/end point Apt ✛ 6C
Lunch Le Fournil, Bonnieux (➤ 100) ✉ 5 place Carnot
☎ 04 90 75 83 62

MONT VENTOUX

The awesome, isolated massif of Mont Ventoux, the "Giant of Provence", rises a lofty 1,912m (6,271ft) above the Plateau de Vaucluse, making it the highest peak between the Alps and the Pyrénées. Italian poet Francesco Petrarch (also known as François Pétrarque) was the first recorded man to reach its summit in 1336. It is a good five-hour hike, but today most people cheat and drive up to the Col des Tempêtes (1,841m/6,038ft). It is important to wrap up warm because Mont Ventoux (Provençal for windy mountain) does indeed do justice to its name. Its bleak limestone peak, totally devoid of vegetation, has been blasted white by icy mistral winds of up to 250kph (155mph). For much of the year, the summit is snow-clad, and skiing on its slopes is a popular pastime.

✚ 6A ❓ Organized hikes to the summit for sunrise (through Bedoin Tourist Office ☎ 04 90 65 63 95; www.bedoin.org)
ℹ Mont Ventoux Information: Chalet d'Accueil du Mont Ventoux, Station du Mont Serein ☎ 04 90 63 42 02

ORANGE

Historic Orange, the "Gateway to Provence", lies in the fertile plain of the Rhône river. Once the Celtic capital of Arausio, later colonized by veterans of the Roman Second Legion, its present name dates from the 16th century, when the town became the property of the House of Orange. Its main claim to fame are two of the finest Roman monuments in Europe – the great triumphal arch and the massive, well-preserved theatre (➤ 54–55). Today Orange is an important centre for Côtes du Rhône wines and produce such as olives, honey and truffles.

The towering 22m high (72ft) **Arc de Triomphe** was the first Roman monument to be built on Gallic soil around 20BC. It was constructed as a symbol of Roman power following Caesar's conquest of the Gauls and victory over the Greek fleet; its archways are covered with intricate carvings depicting naked Gauls bound in chains, victorious Roman legionaries and a variety of nautical symbols. Originally constructed along the Via Agrippa from Lyon to Arles, it now stands on a roundabout in the middle of the N7.

The **Municipal Museum** gives a good insight into life in Roman Gaul. The most remarkable exhibit is a huge marble slab, pieced together from over 400 fragments to create a *plan cadastral* (land survey) of the region, detailing boundaries, land owners and tax rates. The musuem also gives a full history of the city and an introduction to the Théâtre (▶ 54–55).

www.otorange.fr

🚹 3A

ℹ️ 5 cours Aristide-Briand, Orange ☎ 04 90 34 70 88

Arc de Triomphe

✉️ Avenue de l'Arc-de-Triomphe/N7 🎟️ Free

Municipal Museum

✉️ Rue Madeleine-Roch ☎ 04 90 51 17 60

🕐 Jun–Aug daily 9–7; Jan, Feb, Nov, Dec daily 9:30–4:30; Mar, Oct daily 9:30–5:30; Apr, May, Sep daily 9–6 🎟️ Moderate

Théâtre Antique, Orange
Best places to see, ▶ 54–55.

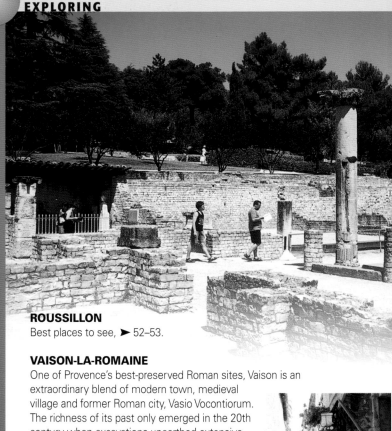

ROUSSILLON
Best places to see, ➤ 52–53.

VAISON-LA-ROMAINE
One of Provence's best-preserved Roman sites, Vaison is an extraordinary blend of modern town, medieval village and former Roman city, Vasio Vocontiorum. The richness of its past only emerged in the 20th century when excavations unearthed extensive **Gallo-Roman remains** including the vast Maison des Messii, with its colonnaded courtyard and mosaic floors, and a Roman theatre (seating 7,000 people during the July arts festival). Visit the Roman city before crossing the 2,000-year-old Pont Romain over the jade-green Ouvèze river.

Clinging to a lofty jagged rock above the river, the sand-coloured houses of Vaison's medieval village, draped with knotted vines, creepers and

pomegranate bushes, have been lovingly restored by artists and craftsmen. The steep climb to the ruined 13th-century château, through a maze of twisting cobbled streets, is rewarded by views of the snow-topped Alps.

www.vaison-la-romaine.com

➕ 5A

🛈 Place du Chanoine-Sautel, Vaison-la-Romaine

☎ 04 90 36 02 11

Gallo-Roman remains

✉ Puymin and La Villasse sites 🕓 Puymin: Apr–Sep 9:30–6; Mar, Oct 10–12:30, 2–5:30; Nov, Dec 10–12, 2–5. La Villasse: Jun–Sep 10–12, 2:30–6:30; Apr, May, 10–12, 2:30–6; Mar, Oct 10–12:30, 2–5:30; Nov, Dec 10–12, 2–5. Closed Jan, Feb 🖐 Apr–Sep expensive; Oct moderate; includes cathedral and cloister

VENASQUE

The lovely ancient village of Venasque, protected by an imposing medieval wall and gateway, enjoys a lofty perch on a steep rock overlooking the Carpentras plain. This formidable site has been occupied since the 6th century, when the bishops of Carpentras sought refuge here from Saracens. It was an episcopal seat for several centuries and a reminder of those times is the 6th-century **baptistry** (renovated in the 11th century), built on the site of a Roman temple dedicated to Venus. The village also has a gastronomic reputation: in May and June there is a daily cherry market, topped off by a cherry festival mid-June.

www.tourisme-venasque.com

➕ 5B

🛈 Grand'Rue, Venasque ☎ 04 90 66 11 66

Baptistière

✉ Place de l'Église ☎ 04 90 66 62 01 🕓 Mid-Jan to mid-Dec daily 9:15–12, 1–6:30 (5 in winter) 🖐 Inexpensive

HOTELS

AVIGNON

Auberge de Cassagne (€€€€)

This 19th-century château, five minutes from Avignon, boasts beautiful gardens, a spa, indoor and outdoor pools and a gastonomic restaurant of international renown.

✉ 450 allée de Cassagne, Le Pontet-Avignon ☎ 04 90 31 04 18; www.aubergedecassagne.com

La Ferme (€€)

Old farmhouse on the Île de la Barthelasse. Rooms are simple but charming, and the island makes for a serene escape from Avignon's summer crowds.

✉ Chemin des Bois, Île de la Barthelasse ☎ 04 90 82 57 53; www.hotel-laferme.com ⏰ Closed Nov to mid-Mar

GORDES

Hôtel Les Bories (€€€)

This top-notch getaway sits just outside of Gordes' old town. Guests can indulge at the hotel's La Maison d'Ennea spa or the on-site gastro-restaurant.

✉ Route de l'Abbaye de Sénanque ☎ 04 90 72 00 51; www.hotellesbories.com

Le Mas de la Beaume (€€€)

A beautiful stone *mas* overlooking the village, with five rooms, a picturesque garden, swimming pool and a Jacuzzi. Serves a fantastic organic farmhouse-style breakfast.

✉ 84220 Gordes Village ☎ 04 90 72 02 96; www.labeaume.com

L'ISLE-SUR-LA-SORGUE

La Maison sur la Sorgue (€€€)

Run by the charming Marie-Claude and Frédéric, these four sumptuous rooms are decorated with treasures sourced from the couple's travels around the world. An excellent breakfast is included in the price.

✉ 6 rue Rose Goudard ☎ 06 87 32 58 68; www.lamaisonsurlasorgue.com

LOURMARIN
Le Paradou (€€–€€€)
Fusing Thai decor within a traditional Provençal bastide, La Paradou's five stunning rooms are set around a natural swimming pool and exotic gardens.

✉ Combe de Lourmarin (D943), route Apt ☎ 04 90 68 04 05; www.hostellerieleparadou.com 🕐 Closed Nov–Mar

MONTEUX
Domaine de Bournereau (€€)
This restored *mas* is a veritable oasis of Provençal calm, with spectacular views of Mont Ventoux, 12 spacious, elegant rooms, extensive gardens and outdoor pool.

✉ 579 Chemin de la Sorguette ☎ 04 90 66 36 13; www.domaine-de-bournereau.com 🕐 Closed Nov–Feb

ROUSSILLON
Hôtel Les Sables d'Ocre (€€)
Tucked in the ochre-stained countryside, this hotel offers basic bedrooms, pretty gardens and a pool. Popular with cyclists.

✉ Les Sablières ☎ 04 90 05 55 55; www.roussillon-hotel.com

VAISON-LA-ROMAINE
Hostellerie le Beffroi (€€)
Atmospheric hotel in Vaison's ancient *haute ville* with cosy rooms. On-site restaurant; in summer meals are served in the garden.

✉ Rue de l'Évêché ☎ 04 90 36 04 71; www.le-beffroi.com 🕐 Closed Jan–Feb

RESTAURANTS

AVIGNON
Christian Étienne (€€€)
One of Avignon's gourmet temples in a 14th-century palace beside the Palais des Papes. Try the summertime Tomato Menu, or splurge on Etienne's exquisite Menu Homard (Lobster Menu).

✉ 10 rue de Mons ☎ 04 90 86 16 50; www.christian-etienne.fr 🕐 Tue–Sat 12:30–2, 7:30–10

Crêperie du Cloître (€)

Savoury or sweet crêpes washed down with a bowl of cider
served up in a picturesque old town square.

✉ 9 place du Cloître-St-Pierre ☎ 04 90 85 34 63 ⏰ Tue–Sat 12–2:30, 7–12

Hiely-Lucullus (€€€)

One of Avignon's top gastronomic palaces: the very upscale decor
is matched by the restaurant's premium cuisine and wine list.

✉ 5 rue de la République ☎ 04 90 86 17 07 ⏰ Daily 12–2, 7–10

Simple Simon (€)

This quaint olde-worlde English tearoom serves steak and kidney
pie, Bakewell tart and even Christmas pudding.

✉ 26 rue Petite-Fusterie ☎ 04 90 86 62 70 ⏰ Mon–Sat 12–7

BONNIEUX
Le Fournil (€€)

A rustic restaurant at the heart of the Lubéron, with a charming
fountain-splashed terrace for alfresco dining.

✉ 5 place Carnot ☎ 04 90 75 83 62 ⏰ Wed–Sun 12–2, 7:30–10:30

CAVAILLON
Prévot (€€€)

Chef Jean-Jaques Prévot's lavish dining room is matched by
equally rich cuisine. Throughout the year, visitors can emulate
Prévot by attending one of his Saturday cooking classes. During
July, the lessons highlight innovative dishes created with Cavaillon
melons, such as *hamburger au melon*.

✉ 353 avenue Verdun ☎ 04 90 71 32 43; www.restaurant-prevot.com
⏰ Tue–Sat 12–1:45, 7:15–9:45

CHÂTEAUNEUF-DU-PAPE
La Mère Germaine (€€)

One of the the village's most popular restaurants in business since
1922. The wine list includes the best *crus* of the appellation.

✉ 3 rue du Commandant-Lemaître ☎ 04 90 83 54 37;
www.lameregermaine.com ⏰ Daily 12–2, 7:30–9:30. Closed Wed in winter

GORDES
Le Mas Herbes Blanches (€€–€€€)
Cambodian–Thai chef Akhara Chay injects a dose of Asian exoticism into Herbes Blanches' Provençal cuisine. During the summer months, be sure to book a table on the panoramic terrace well in advance.

✉ Lieu dit Toron, Joucas ☎ 04 90 05 79 79; www.herbesblanches.com
🕐 Daily 12–1:30, 7–10

Le Mas Tourteron (€€€)
A true taste of Provence in an 18th-century farmhouse, courtesy of Elisabeth Bourgeois' imaginative and refined regional cuisine.

✉ Chemin de Sainte-Blaise-les-Imberts ☎ 04 90 72 00 16 🕐 Wed–Sat 12–2, 7:30–9:30, Sun 7:30–9:30. Closed Nov–Feb

LACOSTE
Café de France (€)
Cheap and cheerful with *salade Niçoise* for under €15, served with a side of priceless views over Bonnieux and the valley beyond.

✉ Le Village ☎ 04 90 75 82 25 🕐 Daily, lunch only

ORANGE
La Roselière (€)
The *saucissons* hanging from the beam overhead become appetizers in this restaurant with a small shady terrace. All dishes are seasonal and homemade.

✉ 4 rue du Renoyer ☎ 04 90 34 50 42 🕐 Thu–Mon 12:30–2:30, 7:30–10

ROUSSILLON
Restaurant David (€€€)
This spot's stunning panoramic terrace juts out between Roussillon's ochre cliffs. Dine on sophisticated Provençal cuisine, such as red mullet poached in fish soup, served with chick pea chips.

✉ Place de la Poste ☎ 04 90 05 60 13; www.le-clos-de-la-glycine.com
🕐 Fri, Sat, Mon, Tue 12–2:30, 7:30–9:30, Sun 12–2:30, Thu 7:30–9:30. Closed mid-Nov to mid-Dec, mid-Jan to mid-Feb.

SEGURET
Le Mesclun (€€)
Intimate restaurant serving regional dishes, carefully paired with
Côtes-du-Rhône wines. Sweeping views of the Comtat Venaissin.
✉ Rue des Poternes ☎ 04 90 46 93 43; www.lemesclun.com 🕓 Wed–Sun
12:30–1:30, 7:30–9

VENASQUE
Auberge de la Fontaine (€€)
A cosy log fire in winter and classical concerts once a month set
the scene for excellent local cooking; try the wild asparagus.
✉ Place de la Fontaine ☎ 04 90 66 02 96; www.auberge-lafontaine.com
🕓 Thu–Tue 7:30–9:30

VIOLÈS
Auberge du Domaine de la Tuilerie (€€)
Both a vineyard and a traditional restaurant, this pretty *auberge*
serves up divine Mediterranean and Provençal dishes.
✉ Violès, west of Gigondas; www.gitesprovence.com ☎ 04 90 70 92 89
🕓 Jul–Aug Wed–Mon 12–3, 8–11; Mar–Jun, Sep–Dec Sat, Sun 12–3, 8–11.
Closed Jan, Feb

SHOPPING

ANTIQUES
Marche´ Antiquit´s & Brocante
One of Provence's finest markets, packed with antiques and
bric-a-brac.
✉ L'Isle-sur-la-Sorgue ☎ Sun 9-6

FOOD AND DRINK
Les Fleurons d'Apt
Using locally-sourced fruits, this factory produces candies,
preserves and jams using traditional methods. Stock up in the
shop, or phone in advance for a factory tour.
✉ N100 (direction Avignon), Apt ☎ 04 90 76 31 43;
www.lesfleurons.apt.com 🕓 Mon–Sat 9–12:30, 2–6; Dec open Sun;
Jan, Feb closed Mon

Les Halles

This modern, covered farmers' market is the perfect place to stock up on goat's cheese, olives and seasonal fruits for a picnic.

✉ Place Pie, Avignon ⏱ Tue–Sun 6am–1:30pm

Les Délices du Lubéron

A tasty selection of olive oil, tapenades, herbs, nougats, candies and other regional products.

✉ 1 Avenue du Partage-des-Eaux, L'Isle-sur-la-Sorgue ☎ 04 90 20 77 37; www.delices-du-luberon.fr ⏱ Daily 10–7

Lou Canesteou

Vaison's best cheese shop, offering a seasonal array of locally made *chèvre* including *banon* (wrapped in chestnut leaves), *picadon* and *cachat*.

✉ 10 rue Raspail, Vaison-la-Romaine ☎ 04 90 36 31 30; www.loucanesteou. com ⏱ May–Sep Mon–Sat 10–7, Sun 10–1; Oct–Apr Tue–Sat 10–7

SPECIALIST
Galerie des Ocres

Ceramics, paintings and gifts created using locally-sourced ochres.

✉ Le Castrum, Roussillon ☎ 04 90 05 62 99; www.galerie-des-acres.fr ⏱ Tue–Sat 10–7

Mouret Chapelier

This milliner has been handcrafting panama hats, Basque berets and Parisian boaters for over 150 years.

✉ 20 rue des Marchands, Avignon ☎ 04 90 85 39 38; www.chapelier.com ⏱ Tue–Sat 9:30–12:30, 2–7

ENTERTAINMENT

NIGHTLIFE
Le Blues

This popular nightclub is home to two dancefloors, each featuring a resident DJ. Music ranges from electro to pop, with monthly themed evenings.

✉ 25 Rue Carnot, Avignon ☎ 06 33 19 55 66; www.leblues.com

Cinéma Utopia

Blockbusters and art-house films, shown in their original language. Additional cinema (one screen) at 5 Rue Figuiére.

✉ 4 Rue des Escaliers Ste-Anne, Avignon ☎ 04 90 82 65 36; www.cinemas-utopia.org/avignon

CLASSICAL ENTERTAINMENT
Opera Théâtre d'Avignon

Concerts by the Orchestra Lyrique de Région Avignon-Provence. Avignon's ballet troop also performs here.

✉ 1 rue Racine, Avignon ☎ 04 90 82 42 42; www.operatheatredavignon.fr

Théâtre Antique

Concerts, opera and theatre in a superb setting (➤ 54–55).

✉ Rue Madeleine Roch, Orange ☎ 04 90 51 17 60; www.theatre-antique.com

COOKING CLASSES
Le Marmiton Cooking School

Some of the regions finest chefs teach one-day, seasonally-themed cooking classes in La Mirande's 19th-century kitchen.

✉ La Mirande, 4 place de la Mirande, Avignon ☎ 04 90 14 20 20; www.la-mirande.fr 🕙 No classes Jul–Aug

SPORTS
Kayak Vert

The scenic Sorgue river is a favourite for canoeing and kayaking.

✉ 84800 Fontaine-de-Vaucluse ☎ 04 90 20 35 44; www.canoefrance.com

Mireio

Explore the Provençal waterways on a scenic river cruise. It's also possible to dine on board.

✉ Allée de l'Oulle, Avignon ☎ 04 90 85 62 25; www.mireio.net

Vélo Loisir en Lubéron

For cyclists in the Luberon region: marked out routes, advice on bike rental, accommodation and restaurants en route.

✉ 203 rue Oscar Roulet, Robion ☎ 04 90 76 48 05; www.veloloisirluberon.com

Marseille and Bouches-du-Rhône

Deep-rooted in the customs of old Provence, this region was the most important part of the Roman Empire outside Italy.

Marseille

Particularly in Arles and Les Baux its monuments, its costumes and its Provençal language have remained well-preserved, while the archeological site of Glanum provides a window onto the region's rich past.

The entire area is scattered with timeless villages, and honey-coloured farmsteads drenched in bougainvillea and oleander. The landscape varies dramatically, from the lacy limestone peaks of the Alpilles and Cézanne's Montagne St-Victoire to van Gogh's nodding sunflower fields. Beyond is the Camargue, a unique nature reserve where pink flamingos, young bulls and semi-wild horses inhabit the marshland.

MARSEILLE

The extraordinary mix of race and culture in France's premier port and oldest city led Alexandre Dumas to describe Marseille as the "meeting place of the entire world". The city has a strong personality, although historcially its reputation edgy. Sporadic gangsterism and racial tension through the 1970s and 80s has been replaced with expanding gentrification, development of Marseille's old docklands and a lively music and contemporary art scene. Marseille is also a traditional city, famous for its shipping, its vegetable oil soap, its *pastis,* the world's largest annual boules competition and the *Marseillaise*. During the French Revolution 500 volunteers were sent from Marseille to Paris – as they marched northwards, they sang a song, composed by Rouget de Lisle in Strasbourg. By the time they reached Paris, it had been adopted as the anthem of the revolution, and was named *La Marseillaise* in honour of the city's "choir". Marseille is a city of contradictions and contrasts, from the bustling downtown districts and vibrant old port to the sandy beaches and chic residences of the Corniche.

For an overview of the city, visit the Musée d'Histiore de Marseille or make time to see some of the city's architectural gems: the Roman and Greek ruins of Marseille's ancient port, the

Jardin des Vestiges, 13th-century Abbaye St-Victor, Cathédrale de la Major (1893), its towering shape based on Istanbul's Hagia Sofia, and Swiss architect Le Corbusier's avant-garde housing project Cité Radieuse (1947–1952), which is now a hotel. Marseille is not an obvious tourist destination and it is admittedly not always easy to find the treasures that lie hidden in this large and vibrant city, but visitors who take the trouble will be richly rewarded.

www.marseille-tourisme.com

✚ 13L

ℹ 4 La Canebière ☎ 04 91 13 89 00 Ⓜ Metro 1: Vieux Port

Basilique de Notre-Dame-de-la-Garde

Marseille's major landmark, standing proudly 162m (531ft) above the city, is a massive neo-Byzantine extravaganza topped by a gilded golden Madonna. The views over the city are unforgettable, as are the model fishing boats and unusual votive offerings painted by fishermen and sailors.

www.notredamedelagarde.com

✚ *Marseille 2d (off map)* ✉ Place Colonel Edon, rue du Fort-du-Sanctuaire ☎ 04 91 13 40 80 🕐 Daily 7–6:15 🚌 60

✋ Free

La Canebière

The main thoroughfare of Marseille took its name from the Provençal *canébe* (cannabis), originally running from former hemp fields to the rope-making heart of the old port. Once considered the Champs Élysées of Marseille, lined with fancy shops, grand cafes and luxury hotels, it remains *the* place for shopping.

✚ *Marseille 3b* Ⓜ Metro 1: Vieux Port; Metro 2 Noailles 🚌 57, 61, 80; trams 1, 2

Château d'If

This forbidding castle lies on the barren, rocky Île d'If, part of the Frioul archipelago. Built in 1524 by François I to protect the port, it later became a prison; its most legendary inmate was Alexandre Dumas' fictional Count of Monte Cristo.

www.if.monuments-nationaux.fr

✚ *Marseille 1c (off map)* ☎ 04 91 59 02 30 🕓 May to mid-Oct daily 9:30–6:30. Closed Mon mid-Sep to Mar 🚢 Frioul If Express: 1 quai Belges ☎ 04 96 11 03 50; www.frioul.cityway.fr ✋ Château: moderate; boat: expensive

Musée Cantini

Former home to artist Jules Cantini, this 17th-century mansion, donated to the city in 1917, houses a permanent collection of 20th-century artworks, including pieces by Picasso and Kandinsky.

✚ *Marseille 3c* ✉ 19 rue Grignan ☎ 04 91 54 77 75 🚇 Metro 1: Estrangin-Préfecture

Bouches-du-Rhône

AIX-EN-PROVENCE

This old capital of Provence still boasts around 40 fountains, a reminder that its name comes from its waters, Aquae Sextiae, as the Romans named it in 122BC. The city thrived culturally during the Middle Ages under Good King René, an ardent patron of the arts, reaching the height of its splendour during the 17th and 18th centuries, with the construction of over 160 *hôtels particuliers* (mansion residences) with beautiful wrought-iron balconies.

www.aixenprovencetourism.com

✚ 13J

🛈 2 place du Général-de-Gaulle, Aix-en-Provence ☎ 04 42 16 11 61

Atelier Paul-Cézanne

Paul Cézanne, Aix's most famous son, spent the last six years of his life working here, painting the rugged limestone hills of the surrounding countryside (➤ 46–47). A special circuit *Cézanne* around town, marked by bronze pavement plaques, leads to the studio – poignantly recreated just as he left it, with reproduction canvases, wine bottles, personal photographs and his old black hat.

www.atelier-cezanne.com

✉ 9 avenue Paul-Cézanne ☎ 04 42 21 06 53 🕓 Daily Jul–Aug 10–6; Apr–Jun, Sep 10–12, 2–6; Oct–Mar 10–12, 2–5 🚌 1 🍽 Cafe (€) 💵 Moderate

Cathédrale St-Sauveur

Aix's main church has a variety of architectural styles: the baptistry is 5th-century, the cloisters Romanesque, the transept and chancel Gothic, and the main portal has magnificently carved walnut Renaissance doors. Don't miss Nicolas Froment's recently restored triptych *Le Buisson Ardent* (1475–6), depicting a vision of the Virgin and Child surrounded by the eternal burning bush of Moses.

✉ Rue de Laroque ☎ 04 42 23 45 65 🕐 Daily 7:30–12, 2–6

Cours Mirabeau

This mansion-lined avenue framed by plane trees, named after the revolutionary Comte de Mirabeau, is centre stage for the wealthy Aixois society who promenade their poodles here between cups of coffee in *Les Deux Garçons* and other Parisian-style cafes. The cours divides the *Vieille Ville* (Old Town) to the north, and the Quartier Mazarin, with its elaborate mansions, to the south.

✉ Cours Mirabeau

Musée Granet

Inside the Gothic priory of the Church of the Knights of Malta, the museum contains 19th-century Aixois artist François Granet's collection of French, Italian and Flemish paintings. There's an impressive sculpture wing on the ground floor and a small collection of modern art upstairs.

www.museegranet-aixenprovence.fr

✉ Place St-Jean-de-Malte ☎ 04 42 52 88 32 🕐 Jun–Sep Tue–Sat 11–7; Oct–May 12–6

LES ALPILLES

South of St-Rémy-de-Provence lies a thirsty landscape of crumpled
white limestone crags – the Chaîne des Alpilles. Market gardens,
vineyards and long avenues of plane trees on the lower slopes
give way to olive groves, and scrub splashed with yellow broom,
lilac lavender and scented wild thyme. This area is easy to explore
on foot, horseback or bike, and you are unlikely to meet anyone
except the occasional flock of sheep.

Often called "the Pompeii of Provence", the ancient ruined
Château of les Baux-de-Provence clings to one of the highest
ridges of the Alpilles. Les Baux is divided into two: the bustling
inhabited lower village, where elegant Renaissance houses line
the shiny cobbled streets, and the deserted Ville Morte perched
above, its ruined buildings hardly distinguishable from the
surrounding limestone crags.

During the Middle Ages, this was the seat of the seigneurs de
Baux, one of southern France's most powerful families. Their cour
d'Amour – a dazzling society of lords, ladies and wandering

troubadours – was renowned throughout the Midi and, ever since, les Baux has been a pilgrimage centre for poets and painters. Today, the windy hilltop redoubt, with its breath-taking panoramic vistas to the sea, is a popular stop for most tourists to the region.

Picturesque Eygalières is off the beaten track, surrounded by a wild, dusty landscape of olive and cypress trees. Its creamy stone houses line the lanes leading up to the village chapel (housing the **Musée du Vieil**), a ruined castle and a panorama of the Alpilles.

www.lesbauxdeprovence.com

➕ 4D

ℹ️ Maison du Roy, Les Baux-de-Provence ☎ 04 90 54 34 39

Château des Baux

✉️ Ville Morte ☎ 04 90 54 55 56; www.chateau-baux-provence.com

🕐 Jul–Aug daily 9–8:30; Apr–Jun 9–6:30; Sep, Oct 9:30–6; Nov–Mar 9:30–5

💷 Moderate ❓ Multi-lingual audioguide included; giftshop

Musée du Vieil

✉️ Chapelle des Pénitents, Eygalières ☎ 04 90 95 91 52 🕐 Mid-Mar to Oct Sun 3–6 💷 Free

ARLES

After centuries of fame, first as the Roman capital of Provence, then as a medieval ecclesiastical centre, Arles seemed content to live on its former glory and fine monuments for many years. Recently, however, it has become a lively, popular city, largely due to a variety of relatively new cultural events, including a renowned photographic fair, a rekindled passion for bullfighting (and bull racing) and the influence of local fashion designer, Christian Lacroix, whose imaginative creations reflect the colourful traditional Arlesian costumes.

For centuries Arles has attracted artists and writers. The beautiful women of the city inspired Daudet's story *L'Arlésienne*, Bizet's opera of the same name and the *farandole*, a medieval dance. Picasso visited to paint the bullfights, and van Gogh moved here in 1888 and lived with Gauguin in the famous yellow house (destroyed in the war), which he immortalized on canvas (*La Maison Jaune*) along with other pictures of Arles including *Café de Nuit* and *Le Pont de Langlois*.

Arles is also surrounded by beautiful, varied countryside, making it the perfect centre for exploring the arid Crau plains, the jagged Alpilles mountains, the fertile banks of the swift Rhône, and the untamed land of the Camargue (➤ 38–39).

www.arlestourisme.com

➕ 3D

ℹ Boulevard des Lices, Arles ☎ 04 90 18 41 20

Les Alyscamps

According to custom, the Roman necropolis of Alyscamps (Latin *elisii campi*, elysian fields) was built outside the city walls along the Via Aurelia. Christians took over the cemetery and several miracles are said to have taken place here, including the appearance of Christ. Burial here was

so sought after that the dead were sealed in barrels and floated down the Rhône to Arles with a piece of gold between their teeth for the gravedigger. At its peak the necropolis had 19 chapels and several thousand tombs – today, it's become a tranquil alleyway lined poplar trees and moss-covered tombs.

✉ Avenue des Alyscamps ☎ 04 90 49 59 05
🕐 May–Sep daily 9–12, 2–7; Mar, Apr, Oct 9–12, 2–6, Nov–Feb 10–12, 2–5 💶 Inexpensive

Arènes

Built during the 1st century AD, this was the largest amphitheatre in Gaul (136m/148 yards long and 107m/117 yards wide), able to seat over 20,000 spectators and scene of blood-thirsty contests between gladiators and wild animals.

Originally it had three storeys, each with 30 marble-clad arcades, and an awning to protect the audience from the elements. During the Middle Ages the stones from the third level were used to build two churches and 200 houses inside the arena to shelter the poor. These were demolished in the 1820s, leaving the amphitheatre once again free for bullfights. During summer, the Arènes stages Wednesday afternoon bull races.

✉ Rond-Point des Arènes
☎ 08 91 70 03 07 🕐 May–Sep daily 9–7 (Wed until 3 Jul–Aug); Mar, Apr, Oct 9–6; Nov–Feb 10–5 💶 Moderate

Église St-Trophime

A masterpiece of Provençal Romanesque, the original church was built in the 5th century, then rebuilt at the end of the 11th century, and the tympanum, depicting the Last Judgement, was added in the next century. By contrast, the austerity of the interior is striking. The cloister of St-Trophime, with rich carvings and sensitively illuminated chapels hung with Aubusson tapestries, is among the treasures of Provence.

✉ Place de la République ☎ 04 90 49 59 05
🕐 Mon–Sat 9–12, 2–6:30, Sun 9–12. Cloister: May–Sep 9–7; Mar, Apr, Oct 9–6; Nov–Feb 10–5
🖐 Church: free; cloister: inexpensive

Espace Van Gogh

It was in Arles that Vincent van Gogh cut off his ear and gave it to a surprised prostitute. He was treated and recovered here, in what was then Arles' local hospital in 1889.

The garden has been restored to match the Dutch artist's descriptions of it during his time here.

www.mediatheque-ville-arles.fr

✉ Place Docteur Félix Rey ☎ 04 90 49 39 39 🕐 Courtyard always open
✋ Free

Musée de l'Arles et de la Provence Antique

This splendid museum is built over the Cirque Romaine, an enormous 2nd-century chariot racecourse, which has recently been excavated. It is a modern museum covering the history of the area from Roman rule to the Christian era.

www.arles-antique.cg13.fr

✉ Presqu'île du Cirque-Romain ☎ 04 90 18 88 88 🕐 Wed–Mon 10–6 ✋ Moderate

Musée Réattu

Previously the 15th-century Grand Priory for the Knights of Malta, this small modern museum has been beautifully restored. The permanent exhibition includes works by Picasso.

www.museereattu.arles.fr

✉ 10 rue du Grand Prieuré ☎ 04 90 49 37 58 🕐 Mar–Sep Tue–Sun 10–7; Oct–Mar 10–12:30, 2–6:30 ✋ Moderate

Théâtre Antique

Fanatical Christians destroyed a large part of the Roman Antique Theatre (1BC): fragments are dotted among the bushes and the flowers. Today the theatre is used for Arles' summer festivals.

✉ Rue de la Calade ☎ 04 90 49 59 05 🕐 May–Sep daily 9–7; Mar, Apr, Oct 9–12, 2–6; Nov–Feb 10–12, 2–5 ✋ Moderate

a walk around Arles

Start in place de la République.

Once the centre of the Roman metropolis, this square is flanked by the Église St-Trophime (➤ 116), the Church of Sainte Anne and the Town Hall.

Leave the square up rue du Cloitre past the Théâtre Antique (➤ 117). Go right into rue de la Calade, anticlockwise around the Arènes (➤ 115) past place de la Major, then turn right down rue Raspail.

Sunny place de la Major, with its tiny Romanesque church, affords sweeping views across the Crau plain to the Alpille hills and is the scene of the famous Fête des Gardians in May (➤ 24).

Cross rue 4-Septembre into rue de Grille towards the Rhône. Turn left along the river bank, keeping the river on your right until you reach place Constantin.

Thermes de Constantin, formerly public baths, were built during the fourth century AD.

Turn left up rue Dominique-Maisto, past the Themes de Constantin on your right, and straight on into rue de l'Hôtel-de-Ville. Turn right at rue des Arènes until you reach place du Forum.

Place du Forum is the heart of Arles and a favourite meeting place for locals and tourists. Note the Corinthian columns embedded into the wall of the Hotel Nord-Pinus (➤ 124).

Leave the square along rue du Palais then turn right into rue Balze past the Cryptoportiques. Bear left at rue Mistral then left into the busy pedestrian shopping street, rue de la République, past Museon Arlaten (currently under restoration until 2013) and back to place de la République.

Distance 2km (1mile)
Time 1 hour/full day with visits
Start/end point Hôtel de Ville, place de la République
Lunch La Paillotte (€) ✉ 28 rue du Dr-Fanton (north of place du Forum) ☎ 04 90 96 33 15

AUBAGNE

This old market town is now virtually a suburb of
Marseille and yet it has preserved its individual charm.
Aubagne is well known for its pottery (the earthenware
figures *santons* originated here) and as the birthplace of
the writer Marcel Pagnol. The films of his famous novels
Jean de Florette and *Manon des Sources* have brought
him to new prominence in recent years. Such sights as
Manon's fountain and Pagnol's grave at la Treille can be
visited by following signed tours into the wild
countryside that surrounds the town.

✚ 14L

🛈 8 cours Barthélémym, Aubagne ☎ 04 42 03 49 98

THE CARMARGUE

Best places to see, ➤ 38–39

CASSIS

This cheerful little fishing port and beach resort basks in
a sheltered bay between the cliffs of the Cap Canaille,
Europe's highest sea cliffs, and the breathtaking
calanques to the west. The surrounding hills are
smothered with olives, almonds, figs, and the terraced
vineyards of the region's highly reputed white wine
(➤ 15). In the village centre, *pétanque* players meet in
dusty squares while fishermen spread their nets along
the bustling quayside, beside its colourful waterfront
cafes. Boat trips leave from a landing stage on the quay.

www.ot-cassis.fr

✚ 14L

🛈 Quai des Moulins, Cassis ☎ 08 92 25 98 92

THE CALANQUES

Best places to see, ➤ 36–37.

MONTAGNE STE-VICTOIRE
Best places to see, ➤ 46–47.

STES-MARIES-DE-LA-MER
This picture-postcard fishing village is steeped in the tradition and folklore of the Camargue (➤ 38–39), with its ancient whitewashed cottages, colourful costumes, bloodthirsty bullfights and flame-red sunsets. According to legend the Virgin Mary's half-sisters Maria Jacobé and Maria Salome landed on the shore here in AD40 with their black serving maid Sarah, patroness of gypsies. When they died a chapel was built over their graves (later replaced by Notre-Dame-de-la-Mer) and the village has been a place of pilgrimage ever since.

The main pilgrimage takes place on 24–25 May. Gypsies, dressed in brightly-painted skirts, shawls, ribbons and flowers, carry statues of the Marias and the bejewelled black Sarah in a small blue boat into the sea to be blessed, led by handsome mounted *gardians* in full costume. There then follows a festival of bullfighting, rodoeos, flamenco and fireworks.

www.saintesmaries.com

✚ 2F

ℹ 5 avenue van Gogh, Ste-Maries-de-la-Mer ☎ 04 90 97 82 55

ST-RÉMY-DE-PROVENCE

Emblematic of Provence's true flavour, St-Rémy is home to warm peaches-and-cream coloured buildings, tree-lined boulevards, fountains, squares and the maze of lanes. Nostradamus was born here in 1503, but today St-Rémy owes its popularity to van Gogh, who convalesced in an asylum just south of town after his quarrel with Gauguin and the ear-cutting incident in Arles. He produced 150 canvases and over 100 drawings during his one year's stay here, including *Starry Night*, *The Sower* and his famous *Irises*.

Near the asylum lie the extensive remains of the wealthy Greco-Roman town of **Glanum**, the oldest classical buildings in France. The area, covering about 2ha (5 acres), was first settled in 6BC and the city was abandoned in the 3rd century when it was overrun by barbarians. Buildings nearby, called Les Antiques, were also part of the Roman town: the oldest and smallest triumphal arch in France, dating from 20BC and the best-preserved mausoleum of the Roman world, erected as a memorial to Caesar and Augustus.

www.saintremy-de-provence.com

✚ 4C

ℹ Place Jean-Jaurès,
St-Rémy-de-Provence
☎ 04 90 92 05 22
Glanum
✉ Route des Baux-de-Provence
☎ 04 90 92 23 79; www.
glanum.monuments-nationaux.fr
🕐 Apr–Sep daily 9:30–6:30
(closed Mon in Sep); Oct–Mar
Tue–Sun 10–5 ✋ Moderate

TARASCON

Most people visit Tarascon, former frontier town of the kingdom of Provence, to see the Renaissance **château** of Good King René, with its moat and turreted towers on the banks of the Rhône. The town is also famous for its dreaded Tarasque, a man-eating monster who, according to legend, was vanquished by the town's patron, Sainte Marthe. At the end of June the green, dragon-like papier-mâché Tarasque parades around town, accompanied by Tartarin, a colourful character created by Alphonse Daudet, who mocks the *petite bourgeoisie* of Provence. This starts four days of festivities, bonfires and bullfights (➤ 25).

www.tarascon.org

✚ 3C

ℹ️ Avenue de la République, Tarascon ☎ 04 90 91 03 52

Château de Tarascon

✉️ Boulevard de Roi-René, Tarascon ☎ 04 90 91 01 93 ⏱ Jun–Sep daily 9:30–6:30; Mar–May, Oct 9:30–5:30; Nov–Feb 9:30–5 💶 Moderate

HOTELS

AIX-EN-PROVENCE
Des Augustins (€€–€€€)
Intriguing blend of history and modernity within a 12th-century former Augustinian convent.

✉ 3 rue de la Masse ☎ 04 42 27 28 59; www.hotel-augustins.com

ARLES
Arlatan (€€–€€€)
This 16th-century residence of the comtes d'Arlatan is a beautiful historic hotel. Rooms and suites decorated with Provençal antiques are set around a courtyard garden and swimming pool.

✉ 26 rue Sauvage ☎ 04 90 93 56 66; www.hotel-arlatan.fr

Hotel Nord-Pinus (€€€)
This hotel is a classified national monument and has strong literary connections; it was once a haunt of Hemingway and Jean Cocteau. Today it is popular with Christian Lacroix, matadors and other wealthy aficionados, and is decorated sumptuously throughout.

✉ Place du Forum ☎ 04 90 93 44 44; www.nord-pinus.com

FONTVIEILLE
Auberge de la Régalido (€€€)
Warm, friendly *auberge* in a converted oil mill, midway between Arles and Les Baux. The hotel is home to an excellent restaurant, leafy gardens, an outdoor pool and a spa.

✉ Rue Frédéric-Mistral ☎ 04 90 54 60 22; www.laregalido.com 🕐 Closed Jan–Feb

MARSEILLE
Le Corbusier (€€–€€€)
Two floors of Swiss architect Le Corbusier's avant-garde housing project, completed in 1952, have been converted into a budget design hotel.

✉ 280 boulevard Michelet, 8e ☎ 04 91 16 78 00; www.hotellecorbusier.com
🚌 21, 22

ST-RÉMY-DE-PROVENCE
Hotel Les Ateliers de L'Image (€€€)
An oasis of sophisticated minimalism at the heart of the town with a tranquil garden, pool and an exotic Franco-Japanese restaurant.

✉ 36 boulevard Victor Hugo ☎ 04 90 92 51 50; www.hotelphoto.com

STES-MARIES-DE-LA-MER
Hotel de Cacharel (€€€)
A former *gardian* ranch in the heart of the marshes. The hotel organizes horseriding excursions through the Camargue.

✉ Route de Cacharel ☎ 04 90 97 95 44; www.hotel-cacharel.com

RESTAURANTS

AIX-EN-PROVENCE
Brasserie Léopold (€€)
Straight out of the belle epoque, this brasserie serves a blend of traditional French and Asian dishes.

✉ 2 avenue Victor Hugo ☎ 04 42 26 01 24; www.hotel-saintchristophe.com
🕓 Daily 12–3, 7–12

La Brocherie (€€)
Try succulent steaks of beef, pork sausage or lamb spit-roasted in the large chimney, or opt instead for the freshly-caught fish at this rustic restaurant. Delicious game in season.

✉ 5 rue Fernand-Dol ☎ 04 42 38 33 21;
www.restaurantlabrocherie-paysaix.com 🕓 Mon–Sat 12–2, 7:30–10

Café des Deux-Garçons (€–€€)
"Les 2 G", founded in 1792, was once the haunt of Cézanne, Picasso, Piaf and Zola. Today, with its original mirrors and chandeliers, it is popular for its brasserie-style menu.

✉ 53 cours Mirabeau ☎ 04 42 26 00 51 🕓 Daily 12–11

Unic Bar (€)
A perfect bar for people-watching, opposite Aix's colourful fruit and vegetable market. In summer, fresh fruit juice is the speciality.

✉ 40 rue Vauvenargues ☎ 04 42 96 38 28 🕓 Daily 6am–2am

ARLES
L'Affenage (€€)
Traditional fare in the converted stables of an 18th-century coaching inn. The abundant hors d'oeuvres buffet is a fine way to sample a large range of local specialities.
✉ 4 rue Molière ☎ 04 90 96 07 67 🕐 Mon–Sat 12–2:30, 7:30–9:30

LES BAUX DE PROVENCE
L'Oustau de Baumanière (€€€)
One of France's finest hotel-restaurants, visited by royalty, politicians and celebrities: the Michelin-starred menus are dusted with foodie gold: truffles, lobster and plenty of foie gras.
✉ Val d'Enfer ☎ 04 90 54 33 07; www.maisonsdebaumaniere.com 🕐 Daily 12–2, 7:30–9:30; Mar, Oct Fri–Tue. Closed Nov, Jan, Feb

CASSIS
Restaurant Chez Gilbert (€€–€€€)
Great bouillabaisse, best paired with a bottle of Cassis' famously crisp white wine. Eat on the terrace overlooking the port.
✉ 19 quai des Baux ☎ 04 42 01 71 36; www.restaurant-chez-gilbert.fr
🕐 Jul, Aug Thu–Tue 12–3, 7–11; Sep–Jun Thu–Tue 12–3, Thu–Mon 7–11. Closed Jan

EYGALIÈRES
Chez Bru (€€)
Imaginative country cooking in this village restaurant includes curry-dressed scallop *carpaccio* with Granny Smith apples, or *wasabi* and basil sorbet.
✉ Route d'Orgon ☎ 04 90 90 60 34; www.chezbru.com 🕐 Mid-Mar to mid-Jan Wed–Sat 12–2, 7:30–9:30, Sun 12–2, Tue 7:30–9:30

MARSEILLE
Le Miramar (€€€)
One of the founding fathers of the elite Marseille Bouillabaisse Charter. Linger over the traditional fish soup alongside the old port.
✉ 12 quai du Port ☎ 04 91 91 10 40; www.bouillabaisse. com 🕐 Tue–Sat 12–2:30, 7:30–9:30 🚇 Metro 1: Vieux Port

Toinou (€–€€)

For towers of the city's freshest seafood, head to this buzzing bistro. Takeaway and delivery also available.

✉ 3 cours St-Louis ☎ 04 91 33 14 94; www.toinou.com 🕔 Daily 11am–11pm 🚇 Metro 1: Vieux Port; Metro 2: Noailles 🚌 57, 61, 80; trams 1, 2

STE-MARIES-DE-LA-MER

Brûleur de Loups (€€)

The tempting menu at this seafront restaurant includes *bourride* (a creamy, garlicky fish soup) and *carpaccio* of Camargue.

✉ 67 avenue Gilbert-Leroy ☎ 04 90 97 83 31 🕔 Tue 12–2:30, Thu–Mon 12–2:30, 7:30–10:30

ST-RÉMY-DE-PROVENCE

Café des Arts (€)

Join the locals in St-Rémy's most popular restaurant for steak with fries, *chevre*-stuffed omlette and frogs' legs.

✉ 30 boulevard Victor-Hugo ☎ 04 90 92 08 50 🕔 Mar to mid-Feb Tue–Sun 8am–11pm

SHOPPING

PROVENÇAL SOUVENIRS AND GIFTS

Bijouterie Pinus

Necklaces, bracelets and crosses in traditional Provençal designs.

✉ 6 rue Jean-Jaurès, Arles ☎ 04 90 96 04 63 🕔 Tue–Sat 9–12, 2:30–7

L'Atelier d'Art

Beautiful southern French ceramics, including Provençal *cigales* (cicadas), pastel vases and olive-embellished egg cups.

✉ 2 boulevard Émile-Combes, Aubagne ☎ 04 42 70 12 92 🕔 Mon–Sat 9–12, 2–6:30

La Compagnie de Provence Marseille

An excellent spot to stock up on Marseille's natural vegetable oil soaps, shampoos and candles.

✉ 18 rue Francis Davso, Marseille ☎ 04 91 33 04 17 🕔 Mon–Sat 10–7–12 🚇 Metro 1: Vieux Port

Les Olivades
Colour-drenched printed fabrics, traditional Provençal clothing and other gift ideas.

✉ Place de la Marie, St-Rémy-de-Provence ☎ 04 90 92 00 80; www.lesolivades.com ⏰ Daily 10–1, 2:30–7. Closed Sun pm and Mon in winter

FASHION
Petit Boy
Fashion for children and teenagers from 6 months to 16 years.

✉ 6 rue Aude, Aix-en-Provence ☎ 04 42 93 13 05

Christian Lacroix
The hometown boutique of the world-famous Arlesian designer.

✉ 52 rue de la République, Arles ☎ 04 90 96 11 16; www.christian-lacroix.fr ⏰ Tue–Sat 10–12, 2–7

FOOD AND DRINK
Chocolaterie Puyricard
Puyricard's handmade chocolates are considered some of the finest in France. Visit their traditional chocolate *atelier*, located in a northern suburb of Aix-en-Provence.

✉ 420 Route du Puy Sainte Réparade, Aix-en-Provence ☎ 04 42 96 11 21; www.puyricard.fr ⏰ Mon–Sat 9–7:30

Distillerie Janot
Janot has been producing Provence's most popular aperitif, *pastis*, since 1928. Tours of the distillery and tastings are by appointment only.

✉ 304 rue du Dirigeable, ZI les Paluds, Aubagne ☎ 04 42 82 29 57; www.janot-distillerie.com ⏰ Mon–Fri 8–12:30, 2–5:30

Le Four des Navettes
Marseille's oldest bakery, founded in 1781. Try the famous orange-flower *navette* biscuits, in the shape of the Stes-Maries' legendary boat (➤ 121), originally only baked during Candlemas, but now available year round.

✉ 136 rue Sainte, Marseille ☎ 04 91 33 32 12; www.fourdesnavettes.com
🕐 Aug daily 9–1, 3–7:30; Sep–Jul Mon–Sat 7am–8pm; Sun 9–1, 3–7:30
🚌 83

ENTERTAINMENT

NIGHTLIFE

Café la Nuit

Popular meeting place at the heart of Arles and subject of a famous van Gogh painting.

✉ 11 place du Forum, Arles ☎ 04 90 49 83 30 🕐 Daily 9am–midnight

El Campo

Bar and restaurant with live entertainment and frequent flamenco shows.

✉ 13 rue Victor-Hugo, Stes-Maries-de-la-Mer ☎ 04 90 97 84 11; www.elcampo.camargue.fr 🕐 Daily 8am–1am. Shows Sat eve in summer

Le Mistral

Join the locals for the latest sounds in techno, house and garage music. Overflowingly popular nightclub.

✉ 3 rue Fréderic-Mistral, Aix-en-Provence ☎ 06 67 46 84 78; www.mistralclub.fr 🕐 Tue–Sun midnight–5am

Le Scat

A live music club with jazz, soul, rhythm and blues, and reggae nights.

✉ 11 rue de la Verrerie, Aix-en-Provence ☎ 04 42 23 00 23 🕐 Tue–Sat 11pm–4am

Trolleybus

Marseille's number one nightlub venue, with DJs, bars and boules.

✉ 24 quai Rive-Neuve, Marseille ☎ 04 91 54 30 45; www.letrolley.com
🕐 Wed–Sat 11:30pm–5am 🚇 Metro 1: Vieux Port

CLASSICAL ENTERTAINMENT

Théâtre Massalia

Marionnette performances, puppetry, circus shows and

contemporary dance, located within La Friche, a former tobacco factory turned arts centre.

✉ La friche la Belle de Mai, 41 rue Jobin, Marseille ☎ 04 95 04 95 70; www.theatremassalia.com 🚌 49, 81

L'Opéra de Marseille

Opera, classical concerts and ballet performances, staged in Marseille's restored opera house.

✉ 2 rue Molière, Marseille ☎ 04 91 55 11 10; www.marseille.fr
Ⓜ Metro 1: Vieux Port

Pavillion Noir

The Ballet Preljocaj performs within this contemporary, architecturally stunning complex.

✉ 530 Avenue Mozart, Ai-en-Provence ☎ 04 42 93 48 80; www.preljocaj.org

SPORTS
A.C.T. Tiki III

Boat trips (1.5 hours) along the Petit Rhone, through the Camargue marshlands. Keep an eye out for flamingos, bulls and herds of horses.

✉ Le Grau d' Orgon, Saintes-Maries-de-la-Mer ☎ 04 90 97 81 68; www.tiki3.fr ⏱ Mid-Mar to Oct

Evana

Guided hikes through the Provençal countryside: explore the Calanques outside Marseille or scale Cézanne's favourite mountain, Sainte Victoire.

✉ 610 Avenue du Général de Gaulle, Eguilles ☎ 04 42 65 83 36; www.evana-provence.com

Les Randonneurs Amis de la Camargue

Horse-riding excursions from two hours to one week. Particularly enjoyable are sunset rides, which include a pause for aperitif.

✉ Route de Cacharel, Saintes-Maries-de-la-Mer ☎ 04 90 97 91 38; www.promenadedesrieges.com

St-Tropez, Var and Haute-Provence

No region of Provence displays such great diversity as the Var, the Alpes-de-Haute-Provence and the Hautes-Alpes. The Var includes Provence's longest coastal strip, wild and rugged with deserted creeks and bleached beaches, far less developed than its famous Riviera neighbour. Its resorts are strung out like pearls along the coast, with St-Tropez the jewel in the crown. Inland, the Var is the most wooded region of France, with sombre green forests of chestnuts, cork oaks and conifers, interrupted only by an occasional yellow splash of mimosa or a quaint, hidden village.

Toulon

In complete contrast, the two mountainous *départements* of Haute-Provence possess some of Provence's most sensational scenery, including Europe's "Grand Canyon", the Gorges du Verdon. Picture-postcard villages and towns, which are rich in Provençal and Alpine architecture, bear witness to a very eventful past, while the mountain air is filled with all the perfumes of Provence.

ST-TROPEZ

Even though the hedonistic image of St-Tropez in the Swinging Sixties has grown distinctly jaded, this charming little fishing port continues to seduce visitors and, despite being a tourist honeypot, remains a magnet for the rich and famous. In the words of the French writer Colette: "Once you have visited here, you will never want to leave."

Most visitors come to St-Tropez to rub shoulders with the glitterati in the waterfront cafes, and admire the grandiose yachts, moored before a backdrop of pink and yellow pastel buildings. Take time to explore the narrow streets and medieval squares of old St-Tropez, where you will find a village of great character with its colourful markets, chic boutiques and romantic bistros. A stroll around the town's main square, the Place du Lices, or a walk through the daily fish market by the harbour, is timeless.

Founded by Greeks as Athenopolis (City of Athena), the town has long been a popular meeting place for artists. Liszt and

Maupassant were its first celebrities in the 1880s, followed by neo-Impressionist painter Signac a decade later. Soon Matisse, Bonnard, Utrillo and Dufy fell under St-Tropez's spell, immortalizing the town on canvas. Many pictures can be seen in the Musée de l'Annonciade (➤ 134).

An influx of writers arrived between the wars, including Colette, Cocteau and Anaïs Nin. Then in the 1950s it was the turn of the film stars, led by Brigitte Bardot. Her scandalous film, *Et Dieu Créa La Femme (And God Created Woman)* of 1956, marked the start of a permissive era and the Bardot/St-Tropez cult.

St-Tropez's star-studded list of residents includes Elton John, George Michael, Jean-Paul Belmondo and Jean Michel Jarre and, although it may no longer be how it was in its heyday, everything here is still extravagant, decadent, excessive. Little wonder the French endearingly call it St "Trop" ("too much").

www.ot-saint-tropez.com

✚ 19L

ℹ Quai Jean-Jaurès, St-Tropez ☎ 04 94 97 45 21

La Citadelle

Visit this 16th-century hilltop fortress if only for the view, which embraces the orange, curly-tiled roofs of St-Tropez's *vieille ville*, the dark and distant Maures and Esterel hills, and the glittering blue of the bay. The citadel contains a fascinating historical display illustrating the town's long and glorious history. Children will enjoy a visit here, racing back and forth over the drawbridge and around the castle grounds.

✉ Montée de la Citadelle ☎ 04 94 97 06 53 🕐 Apr–Sep daily 10–6:30; Oct–Mar 10–12:30, 1:30–5:30 ✋ Inexpensive

Église St-Tropez

St-Tropez owes its name to a Roman centurion called Torpes, who was martyred under Nero in AD68. His head was buried in Pisa and his body put in a boat with a dog and cockerel who were to devour it. However, when the boat washed up here, his remains were miraculously untouched. For over 400 years the town's most important festival – the Bravade de St-Torpes – has been celebrated in his honour. You can see a gilt bust of St Torpes and a model of his boat in the 19th-century church, with its distinctive pink and yellow bell-tower.

✉ Rue de l'Église 🕐 Daily

Musée de l'Annonciade

This former 16th-century chapel houses late 19th- and early 20th-century French paintings and bronzes. St-Tropez was then one of the most active centres of avant-garde art and, as a result, most of the 100 or so canvases belong to the pointillism,

fauvism and nabism movements. Many of the paintings portray local scenes. Look for Paul Signac's *L'Orage* (1895), Bonnard's *Le Port de St-Tropez* (1899), Camoin's *La Place des Lices* (1925), works by Dufy, Derain, Matisse, Maillol, Vuillard and others.

✉ Place Georges-Grammont ☎ 04 94 17 84 10
🕐 Jun–Sep Wed–Mon 10–12, 3–7; Oct–May Wed–Mon 10–12, 2–6; closed Nov
✋ Moderate

Place des Lices

This is the real heart of St-Tropez, and remains very much as it looked in Camoin's 1925 *La Place des Lices* (➤ 134), lined with ancient plane trees and bohemian cafes. The best time to visit is on Tuesdays or Saturdays for its colourful market, but come anytime for a game of boules and a glass of *pastis* with the locals.

✉ Place des Lices

🍴 Le Café (➤ 156)

St-Tropez Beaches

St-Tropez's best private beaches are along the Baie de Pampelonne, a peninsula with over 6km (4 miles) of golden sand, neatly divided into individual beaches. The best public beaches on the peninsula are Plage Gigaro and Plage du Débarquement.

Le Club 55 ✉ Boulevard Patch ☎ 04 94 55 55 55; **Tahiti-Plage** ✉ Route de Tahiti ☎ 04 94 97 18 02; **La Voile Rouge** ✉ Route des Tamaris ☎ 04 94 79 84 34 🚌 Shuttle buses operate between the place des Lices (➤ above) and all the beaches listed above in summer

Vieux Port

Artists and writers have been enticed to the pretty pastel-painted houses and crowded cafes that line the quay for over a century. Today, the waterfront is very much the place to see and be seen in St-Tropez, so try to arrive in your Aston Martin, on your Harley Davidson, or better still in an enormous floating gin palace. It's also fun to simply wander along the quayside, marvelling at the size and cost of these ostentatious yachts.

✉ Vieux Port

a walk around St-Tropez

Start on the waterfront beside the Tourist Office. Go through the Porte de la Poissonnerie, past the daily fish market into place aux Herbes.

A stone's throw from the glamour of the quayside, the colourful daily fish, fruit and vegetable stalls remind visitors of St-Tropez's modest village past.

Leave the square up the steps of rue du Marché, turn left into rue des Commerçants, first right into rue du Clocher to Église St-Tropez (► 134). Continue along rue Cdt-Guichard to place de la Mairie, dominated by its handsome pink and green town hall, and place Garrezio.

The massive tower is all that remains of St-Tropez's oldest building, 10th-century Château de Suffren, once home of the locally-born 18th-century seaman Admiral Suffren.

Return past the town hall and along rue de la Ponche. The 15th-century Porche de la Ponche archways lead to the old Ponche quarter.

This is the old fishing district of St-Tropez, centred on the sun-baked place du Revelin, overlooking the unspoiled fishing port and tiny shingle beach, where locals still take a dip each morning.

Head up rue des Ramparts, right at rue d'Aumale to the delightful place de l'Ormeau, and left up rue de l'Ormeau to rue de la Citadelle. Proceed downhill towards the port, taking the first left turn into rue Portail Neuf as far as the chapel.

The Chapelle de la Miséricorde with its quaint bell-tower dates from the 17th century and the road alongside passes through its flying buttresses. The chapel's entrance is on rue Gambetta.

Continue along rue Gambetta for lunch in place des Lices (➤ 135).

Distance 1.5km (1 mile)
Time 1–1.5 hours, depending on church visits
Start point Waterfront
End point Place des Lices
Lunch Le Café (➤ 156) ✉ Place des Lices ☎ 04 94 97 44 69

The Var

AUPS

The peaceful walled village of Aups basks in a wide valley, backed by undulating hills smothered in vines and olives. The village has a local reputation for its wine, honey, oil, black truffles and other regional specialities sold at the local Thursday-morning market. With its friendly folk, medieval gateways, shady streets, small squares dotted with fountains and a charming little museum of modern art in an old converted convent, Aups offers the perfect getaway.

www.aups-tourisme.com

✠ 17J

🛈 Place Frédéric-Mistral, Aups ☎ 04 94 84 00 69

BORMES-LES-MIMOSAS

Despite a chequered history – founded by the Gauls, conquered by the Romans, then variously sacked by Saracens, Corsairs, Moors, Genoese and finally during the Wars of Religion – this hillside village remains one of the prettiest of the entire coast. Its ice-cream coloured pantiled houses spiral down steep stairways and alleys, with amusing names – Lover's Lane (Venelle des Amoreux), Gossipers Way (Draille des Bredovilles) and steepest of all, Bottom-Breaker Road (Roumpi-Crou). Depending on the season, Bormes is bathed in the scent of mimosa, eucalyptus, oleander and camomile. In February, when the mimosa is in full bloom, it celebrates with its sensational *corso fleuri* – an extravaganza of floral floats made from myriads of tiny yellow flowers.

A *circuit touristique* that starts at the Maisons des Associations on boulevard de la Republique embraces most of the sights, including a fine 16th-century chapel dedicated to St François-de-Paule, an 18th-century church built in Romanesque style, a

museum of local art, and a ruined fortress with amazing views

www.bormeslesmimosas.com

✚ 18M

🛈 9 place Gambettat, Bormes-les-Mimosas ☎ 04 94 01 38 38

COGOLIN

Old Cogolin, with its brightly coloured medieval houses, narrow cobbled streets and peaceful hidden *placettes* (tiny squares), offers a welcome escape from the crowds of nearby St-Tropez. Cogolin's economy depends on the traditional crafts of making cane furniture, silk yarn, briar pipes, knotted wool carpets and above all, reeds for wind instruments, attracting musicians of renown.

www.cogolin-provence.com

✚ 19L

🛈 Place de la République, Cogolin ☎ 04 94 55 01 10

COLLOBRIÈRES

The tranquil village of Collobrières lies alongside the Collobrier river at the heart of the wild Massif des Maures, surrounded by densely forested hillsides of cork oaks and chestnut trees bearing fruits the size of tennis balls. Collobrières is reputed to have been first in France to learn about corkage from the Spanish in the Middle Ages and cork production is still the major industry, together with *marrons glacés* and other sweet chestnut confectionery.

www.collobrieres-tourisme.com

✝ 18L

🛈 Boulevard Charles-Caminat, Collobrières ☎ 04 94 48 08 00

CORNICHE DE L'ESTEREL

In stark contrast to the over-developed resorts to the east, the Corniche de l'Esterel coast remains the sole stretch of wild coast left between St-Raphaël and Théoule-sur-Mer: a ragged shoreline of startlingly red cliffs, tumbling into a bright blue sea from the craggy wilderness of the Massif de l'Esterel beyond, piercing the coast with tiny deserted bays. The narrow road twists along the coast, dipping down through some of the region's least pretentious resorts. Inland, the blood-red porphyry mountains of the Massif, for centuries the haunt of bandits, are smothered in brilliant green spruce, pine and scrub, and summer wild flowers.

✚ 21K

FRÉJUS

The oldest Roman city in Gaul, founded by Julius Caesar in 49BC, the flourishing naval town of Fréjus (Forum Julii) lay on the Aurelian Way from Rome to Arles. The fragile 1st- to 2nd-century **Roman arena** and theatre are still used for bullfights and concerts, and the Provençal cathedral contains one of France's oldest baptistries, perfectly preserved and dating from the 4th or 5th century. Following the decline of the Roman Empire, the port lost its significance and eventually silted up, forming the beaches of Fréjus-Plage, a resort that merges into St-Raphaël.
www.frejus.fr

✚ 20K

🛈 325 rue Jean-Jaurès ☎ 04 94 51 83 83

Arène Frèjus

☎ 04 94 51 34 31 🕓 May–Oct Tue–Sun 9:30–12:30, 2–6; Nov–Apr Tue–Sun 9:30–12:30, 2–5 ✋ Free

GRIMAUD

One of Provence's most photogenic hilltop villages, Grimaud is crowned by a ruined 11th-century château belonging to the Grimaldi family, after whom the village is named. By contrast, Port-Grimaud on the coast is a modern mini-Venice of designer villas lining the quayside. Designed by François Spoerry in the 1960s, it is best viewed by renting a boat or climbing the church tower.

www.grimaud-provence.com

✚ 19L ❓ Tourist train links Port-Grimaud to the hilltop village of Grimaud

ℹ 1 boulevard des Alziers, Grimaud ☎ 04 94 55 43 83

HYÈRES

The oldest of the Côte d'Azur winter resorts, Hyères-les-Palmiers is so-called because of its important palm-growing industry. Its popularity in the early 20th century had faded by the end of the century because it is 4km (2 miles) inland and not actually on the newly fashionable seaside. Hyères' main attraction lies 10km (6 miles) off the Var coast – the three islands of the Îles d'Hyères.

www.hyeres-tourisme.com

✚ 17M 🚢 Ferries depart Port de la Tour-Fondue, Presquîle de Giens 3–5 times daily for the Îles d'Hyères, hourly in summer ☎ 04 94 58 21 81; www.tlv-tvm.com

ℹ Avenue Ambroise Thomas ☎ 04 94 01 84 50

The Alpes-de-Haute-Provence

COLMARS

The name Colmars stems from Roman times when a temple to the god Mars was erected on the hill (Collis Martis), which today forms the backdrop to this small fortified village. Hidden in a high wooded valley of the Haut-Verdon, amid the highest peaks of the Alpes-de-Haute-Provence, the wooden alpine chalets, with their sloping roofs and balconies crimsoned with geraniums, seem far removed from the stone *mas* of the Var. It is here that the kingdom of France once bordered Savoy, hence the impregnable walls and two massive medieval castles, which crown the village and guard the bridges at either end. The northern **Fort de Savoie** is the more imposing and contains a cultural centre where exhibtions are held in the summer.

www.colmars-les-alpes.fr

✚ 27T

ℹ Ancienne Auberge Heurie ☎ 04 92 83 41 92

Fort de Savoie

🕐 Jul–Aug 2:30–7 ✋ Moderate

DIGNE-LES-BAINS

This genteel town and departmental capital in the pre-Alps beside the Bléone river, lies on the Route Napoléon, which was used by the emperor after his escape from Elba. Its sheltered location, mild sunny climate, invigorating air and the thermal springs to the south of town have made it a renowned spa. The town's other main attraction is lavender. This aromatic plant has been used since the Middle Ages for its therapeutic qualities, and Digne is the lavender-growing capital of Provence with an annual *corso de la lavande* (➤ 24) at the start of August. The Route de la Lavande passes through Digne and takes in the area's main lavender producing places. Digne marks the end of Le Train des Pignes ("Pinecone" line), an old train that runs through the mountain valleys to Nice.

www.ot-dignelesbains.fr

✚ 10A ☐ Pinecone line ☎ 04 92 31 01 58 (Digne); 04 97 03 80 80 (Nice); www.trainprovence.com

ℹ Rond-Point du 11-Novembre 1918, Digne-les-Bains ☎ 04 92 36 62 62

ENTREVAUX

Sleepy Entrevaux was once an important border defence between France and Savoy, heavily fortified in the 1690s by Vauban, Louis

XIV's military architect. Enter the village across a drawbridge, through one of three gatehouses into a hotchpotch of typical Provençal medieval houses, surprisingly untouched by the proximity of the Alps. The steep path to the citadel is well worth the climb for the views of the Haut-Var and the mountains. www.entrevaux.info

✚ 20G ⊙ Citadel open 24 hours by electronic ticket gate ✋ Inexpensive
ℹ Porte Royale, Entrevaux ☎ 04 93 05 46 73 ⊙ Summer only

FORCALQUIER

This old market town is situated on the Roman Via Domita, which linked the Alps with the Rhône delta. It takes its name from the limestone kilns *(furni calcarii)* which the Romans hewed into the hillside. During the Middle Ages it was a powerful town and seat of the counts of Provence. On one occasion all four kings visited Forcalquier simultaneously and the region was dubbed the "land of the four queens". The surrounding countryside is particularly lush and beautiful. According to the nearby **Observatory of Haute Provence,** it has the cleanest, clearest air of anywhere in France, and makes a good base to explore the hilltop villages of Limans, Banon, Dauphin and Simiane-la-Rotonde.

www.forcalquier.com

✚ 8B
ℹ 13 place Bourguet ☎ 04 92 75 10 02

Observatoire de Haute Provence
✉ St-Michel ☎ 04 92 70 64 00; www.obs-hp.fr ⊙ Jul–Aug Mon, Wed, Thu 1:30–4:30; May, Jun, Sep–Nov Wed 2–4 ✋ Moderate
❓ Guided tours only

GORGES DU VERDON

Best places to see, ➤ 44–45.

GRÉOUX-LES-BAINS

Europe's oldest spa town lies in a beautiful, lavender- and thyme-scented valley above the Verdon river, making it a perfect excursion base for outdoor sports, especially walking, cycling and fishing. Try its warm sulphurous waters used since Roman times for treating arthritis, rheumatism and respiratory problems.

www.greoux-les-bains. com

✚ 9D

🛈 5 avenue des Marronniers, Gréoux-les-Bains

☎ 04 92 78 01 08

MOUSTIERS-STE-MARIE

Dramatically perched high on a ridge surrounded by sheer cliffs, Moustiers marks the start of the great gorges of the Verdon river (➤ 44–45). In the 17th and 18th centuries its white decorated earthenware pottery was famous throughout the world. Now *Faïence de Moustiers* has been revived and is sold in countless craft shops in every cobbled square.

The 5th-century chapel of Notre-Dame-de-Beauvour is pinned against the rockface at the top of the village. Above it hangs a renowned gold star, suspended on a 227m (745ft) chain, presented to the village by a knight called Blacas to celebrate his release from captivity during a crusade.

www.moustiers.eu

✚ 11C

🛈 Place de l'Eglise, Moustiers-Ste-Marie ☎ 04 92 74 67 84

LES PENITENTS DES MÉES

An extraordinary feature marks the entry into the Durance valley from Digne and the Provençal Alps – curiously eroded limestone pinnacles, which stand tightly packed together and tower 150m (492ft) above the village of Les Mées (named after the Latin *metae*, milestone). According to a 5th-century legend, the pinnacles were formed when local monks were attracted to some beautiful Moorish girls who were captured by a knight during the Saracen invasions. Disgraced, the monks were banished from the village and, in punishment, turned to stone.

✚ 9B

🛈 Boulevard de la République, Les Penitents des Mées ☎ 04 92 34 36 38

The Hautes-Alpes

BRIANÇON

This fortified city stands amid the snow-capped peaks of the southern Alps, and combines a rich historical past with an easy-going Provençal lifestyle. In summer the surrounding countryside is a hikers' paradise, and in winter Serre-Chevalier, one of France's top ski resorts, provides 250km (155 miles) of challenging slopes.

www.ot-briancon.fr

✚ 27N

ℹ 1 place Temple, Briançon ☎ 04 92 21 08 50

EMBRUN

Gateway to the wild Queyras and the lofty Ecrins mountains, this colourful town was once an important episcopal seat. Its former cathedral, one of the finest churches in the French Alps, has beautiful Renaissance stained glass and one of the oldest organs in France.

✚ 27R

🛈 Place Général-Dosse, Embrun ☎ 04 92 43 72 72

GAP

This lively town and capital of the Hautes-Alpes, between Provence and the mountains of the Dauphiné, is popular for both summer and winter sports.

www.gap-tourisme.fr

✚ 25R

🛈 2a cours Frederic Mistral, Gap ☎ 04 92 52 56 56

LA GRAVE

One of the oldest and most important mountaineering stations in France, on the northern edge of the Hautes-Alpes. La Grave sits opposite the imposing peak of la Meije (3,983m/1,3064ft), a great challenge for climbers.

www.lagrave-lameije.com

✚ 26N

🛈 RN91, La-Grave-La Meijie ☎ 04 76 79 90 05

ST-VÉRAN

The highest village in Europe at 2,040m (6,691ft), St-Véran is a few wooden chalets dotted over a mountainside. A track leads through pastures sprinkled with mountain flowers to the tiny chapel of Notre-Dame-de-Clausis, object of a pilgrimage every July.

www.saintveran.com

✚ 28Q

🛈 St-Véran ☎ 04 92 45 82 21

SISTERON

Sitting high on a rocky bluff, the grandiose **citadel** of Sisteron
(12th–16th century) dominates an unusually varied landscape, with
the harsh Dauphiné mountains to the north and a rich valley to the
south. The strategic importance of the town was emphasized as
recently as 1944 when it suffered Allied air attacks. The citadel's

guardroom contains a museum of local wartime resistance.

www.sisteron.fr

🕂 9A

🛈 Place de la République, Sisteron ☎ 04 92 61 12 03

La Citadelle

☎ 04 92 61 27 57 🕔 Jun–Sep 9–7, Apr–May, Oct–Nov 9–5 ✋ Moderate

HOTELS

BANDOL
Golf Hotel (€€)

Cosy, inexpensive beachside property with two dozen rooms and free parking. Family rooms available.

✉ Plage de Rènecros ☎ 04 94 29 45 83; www.golfhotel.fr ⏱ Closed mid-Oct to mid-Mar

BORMES LES MIMOSAS
Le Bellevue (€€)

A handsome yet simple establishment on Bormes' main square.

✉ 12 place Gambetta ☎ 04 94 71 15 15; www.bellevuebormes.com
⏱ Closed Dec

FAYENCE
Moulin de la Camadoule (€€€)

A renovated mill with a dozen rooms, nestled in acres of orchards along with a restaurant and swimming pool.

✉ Chemin Notre Dame ☎ 04 94 76 00 84; www.camandoule.com

FORCALQUIER
Charembeau (€€)

Heartily recommended family-run hotel with traditional Provençal features throughout. Family rooms available.

✉ Route de Niozelles ☎ 04 92 70 91 70; www.charembeau.com ⏱ Closed mid-Nov to Jan

GRÉOUX-LES-BAINS
Villa Borghese (€€€)

A delightful hotel with flower-filled balconies, a garden and pool.

✉ Avenue des Thermes ☎ 04 92 78 00 91; www.villa-borghese.com
⏱ Closed Jan–mid-Mar

MONÊTIER-LES-BAINS
L'Auberge du Choucas (€€€)

Cosy farmhouse in the Alps, and ideal for skiing at Serre Chevalier.

✉ Monêtier-les-Bains ☎ 04 92 24 42 73; www.aubergeduchoucas.com

MOUSTIERS-STE-MARIE
La Bonne Auberge (€–€€)
Clean, modest hotel near the great Verdon gorges.
✉ Route de Castellane ☎ 04 92 74 66 18; www.bonne-auberge-moustiers.com 🕒 Closed Nov–Mar

ST-TROPEZ
Château de la Messardiere (€€€€)
One of St-Tropez's most luxurious hotels, with a spa and extensive grounds. Truly palatial.
✉ Route de Tahiti ☎ 04 94 56 76 00; www.messardiere.com 🕒 Closed Dec–Feb

Pastis (€€€€)
St-Tropez's newest and most chic offering, wtih nine boutique rooms set around a black swimming pool.
✉ 61 avenue du Général Leclerc ☎ 04 98 12 56 50; www.pastis-st-tropez.com 🕒 Closed Dec

Villa Marie (€€€€)
On the hill overlooking Pampelonne, this chic boutique hotel and spa, stylishly decorated with terracotta, wrought iron and St-Tropez azure, is *the* address for the beautiful people.
✉ Chemin Val de Rien, Ramatuelle, near St-Tropez ☎ 04 94 97 40 22; www.villamarie.fr

ST-VÉRAN
Les Chalets du Villard (€€)
Alpine chalet accommodation in the highest village in Europe.
✉ Le Villard ☎ 04 92 45 82 08; www.leschaletsduvillard.fr 🕒 Closed mid-Apr to mid-Jun, mid-Sep to mid-Dec

TOURETTES
Four Seasons Provence (€€€€)
Beautifully tended country resort and golf complex. The hilltop villas and restaurants are set to resemble a Provençal village.
✉ Terre Blanche ☎ 04 94 39 90 00; www.fourseasons.com/provence

RESTAURANTS

BORMES-LES-MIMOSAS
Lou Portaou (€€)
Hidden in a picturesque corner of Bormes, this small restaurant serves a simple menu of market-fresh Provençal cuisine. The set menus are very good value.

✉ 1 rue Cubert-des-Poètes ☎ 04 94 64 86 37 🕐 Jan to mid-Nov Wed–Mon 12–1:30, 7–9:30

COLLOBRIÈRES
La Petite Fontaine (€)
Try some local delicacies of the Massif des Maures, washed down with wine from the local cooperative on a shady terrace. Peaceful.

✉ 1 place de la République ☎ 04 94 48 00 12 🕐 Tue–Sun 12–2:30, 7–10, Sun 12–2:30

DIGNE-LES-BAINS
Le Grand Paris (€€)
With the reputation of Digne's best restaurant, in a former 17th-century convent. Try the roast seabass in a bouillabaisse sauce, or local rabbit and beef.

✉ 19 boulevard Thiers ☎ 04 92 31 11 15; www.hotel-grand-paris.com 🕐 Mar–Nov daily

La Taverne (€)
The hippest eatery in Digne dishes up salads, pizza and giant sharing platters of seafood and grilled meat.

✉ 36 boulevard Gassendi ☎ 04 92 31 30 82 🕐 Daily 11:30–3, 6:30–midnight

FAYENCE
Le Castelleras (€€€)
Roast duckling in apple and orange sauce, or langoustine and scallop kebabs, are just two of the specialities served in this old stone *mas*.

✉ Route de Seillans ☎ 04 94 76 13 80; www.restaurant-castelleras.com 🕐 Mid-Feb to mid-Jan Wed–Sun 12–2:30, 7–9:30

FORCALQUIER
Terrasses de la Bastinde (€€)

Traditional cuisine from Savoy and Provence from heavy cheese dishes to roast pigeon.

✉ Restanque de Beaudines ☎ 04 92 73 32 35 ⏰ Mid-Jun to mid-Sep 12–2, 7–10; mid-Sep to mid-Jun Wed–Sat 12–2, 7-10, Tue 7–10, Sun 12–2

GAP
Le Tourton des Alpes (€€)

The local speciality of *tourtons* – tiny hot pastry envelopes filled with either potato, spinach, meat, prune or apple – are served here in copious quantities.

✉ 1 rue des Cordiers ☎ 04 92 53 90 91 ⏰ Daily

GRIMAUD
Les Santons (€€)

Classic cuisine and impeccable service in elegant Provençal surroundings.

✉ Route Nationale ☎ 04 94 43 21 02 ⏰ Fri–Tue 12–2, 7:30–10

HYÈRES
Bistrot de Marius (€€)

Dine in the romantic interior or on the outdoor tables, which occupy an entire corner of Hyères' main square. Beautifully presented local meats and fish, with great value set menus.

✉ 1 place Massillon ☎ 04 94 35 88 38; www.bistrotdemarius.fr ⏰ Jul–Aug Tue–Sun 12–2, 7–10; Jan–Jun, Sep, Oct Wed–Sun

MOUSTIERS-STE-MARIE
La Bastide de Moustiers (€€€)

Dine in the country home of one of the world's top culinary artists, Alain Ducasse. Head chef Alain Souliac weaves together southern French flavours from strawberries to courgette flowers and Sisteron lamb.

✉ Chemin de Quinson, 04360 la Grisolière ☎ 04 92 70 47 47; www.bastide-moustiers.com ⏰ Apr–Oct daily 12–2, 7:30–9:30; Mar, Nov, Dec Thu–Mon

Les Santons (€€)

Well-priced local cuisine from sander in fennel sauce to roast lamb with ratatouille served in delightful surrounds. Outdoor terrace.

✉ Place de l'Église ☎ 04 92 74 66 48; www.lessantons.com ◷ Mid-Feb to mid-Nov Wed–Sun 12–2, 7–9, Mon 12–2 (Jul–Aug closed Mon and Sat lunch)

SISTERON
Hotel Restaurant de la Citadelle (€)

Enjoy a spectacular alpine panorama whilst trying local delicacies such as confit of lamb baked for seven hours, or blueberry tart. Bargain lunchtime menus.

✉ 126 rue Saunerie ☎ 04 92 61 13 52 ◷ Daily 12–2:30, 7–10

ST-TROPEZ
Le Café (€€)

This famous meeting spot of artists and intellectuals, formerly known as the Café des Arts, has a hip history – Mick Jagger's wedding reception was held here in 1971. An archetypal French bar, perfect for sipping espresso or a glass of *pastis.*

✉ Place des Lices ☎ 04 94 97 44 69; www.lecafe.fr ◷ Daily 8am–midnight

La Ponche (€€)

On a tranquil terrace by St-Tropez's tiny town beach, this seafood restaurant plies local bass and bream, oysters, scallops and lobster.

✉ Rue des Remparts ☎ 04 94 97 09 29; www.laponche.com ◷ Apr–Sep daily 12–3, 7–11

Salama (€€)

Superb Moroccan restaurant in a quiet alley by place du Lices. Try *tajines* brimming with lamb, spices, fruit and nuts.

✉ 1 rue Tisserands ☎ 04 94 97 59 62 ◷ Jun–Aug daily 7–11; Mar–May, Sep Tue–Sun 7–11

Le Sporting (€€)

Local favourite on bustling place du Lices. Good value lunches and dinners include pizza, moules-frites and speciality hamburgers.

✉ Place des Lices ☎ 04 94 97 00 65 ◷ Daily 7–midnight

La Table du Marché (€€)

This smart bistro-cum-deli offers an array of light snacks, regional specialities, pastries, cakes and wines all overseen by celebrity French chef Christophe Leroy. There's a good value set menu in the evening, made from fresh market produce.

✉ 38 rue Georges Clemenceau ☎ 04 94 97 85 20;
www.christophe-leroy.com ⏰ Daily 12:30–3, 7–11

THÉOLE-SUR-MER
La Marine (€€)

Possibly the best sardines on the Corniche de l'Esterel, on a breezy terrace overhanging the Mediterranean.

✉ Port de Miramar ☎ 04 93 75 49 30 ⏰ Closed out of season

SHOPPING

PROVENÇAL SOUVENIRS AND GIFTS
Aim

Stumble across four stores within tiny Ramatuelle's city walls. Gifts include homewear, modern art, bedspreads and ceramics.

✉ Ramatuelle ☎ 06 11 62 01 63

FASHION
Hermès

The ultimate in French chic.

✉ Place Grammond, St-Tropez ☎ 04 94 97 04 29 ⏰ Tue–Sat 10–12:30, 2:30–7:30

Rondini

The makers of Tropézienne sandals, the essential St-Trop footwear favoured by the likes of Picasso.

✉ 16 rue Georges Clemenceau, St-Tropez ☎ 04 94 97 19 55

FOOD AND DRINK
Maison des Confitures

A huge variety of preserves from pinenut jam to carrot chutney.

✉ Route du Bourraine, Gassin ☎ 04 94 43 41 58;
www.maisondesconfitures.com ⏰ Mon–Sat 9:30–7

Pain d'Epicerie
Jars of local preserves, mountain honey and home-made liqueurs.
✉ Rue de Marché, Entrevaux ☎ 04 93 05 49 89

Petit Village
Stocks the wines of the Mâitres Vignerons of St-Tropez at this manmoth wine shop.
✉ Carrefour de la Foux, route Cogolin, Gassin ☎ 04 94 56 40 17;
www.terres-de-mer.com ⏰ Mon–Sat 8:30–12:30, 2:30–7

La Tarte Tropézienne
The original inventors of Brigitte Bardot's favourite tart, a sponge-cake sandwich filled with custard cream. One of several branches around the town.
✉ 36 rue Georges Clemenceau, St-Tropez ☎ 04 94 97 71 42

ENTERTAINMENT

NIGHTLIFE
Les Caves du Roy
St-Tropez's spiciest nightspot and a haven for A-list celebs.
✉ Hotel Byblos, avenue Paul-Signac, St-Tropez ☎ 04 94 97 16 02;
www.lescavesduroy.com ⏰ Easter–Oct 11pm–5am

VIP Room
A star-studded nightclub – the hangout of St-Tropez's gilded youth.
✉ Boulevard 11-Novembre 1918, St-Tropez ☎ 04 94 97 14 70 ⏰ Daily;
weekends only in winter

SPORTS
Serre Chevalier
Provence's premier Alpine ski resort, near Briançon.
☎ 04 92 24 98 98; www.serre-chevalier.com

Gap Bayard
One of the largest *ski-de-fond* (cross-country skiing) regions in the Hautes-Alpes.
☎ 04 92 50 16 83; www.gap-bayard.com

Nice and Alpes-Maritimes

This dramatic stretch of vivid blue coastline with its chic cities, sandy beaches, craggy corniches and fishing villages has long attracted a rich assortment of actors, artists, writers and royalty to its shores. The luxury boutique hotels, designer shops and terrace cafes of the smartest Riviera resorts – Cannes, Nice and Monaco – exude a carefree *joie de vivre*, basking in the scorching Mediterranean sun, while their ports overflow with millionaires' yachts. After all, this is the home of the rich and famous – the world's most sophisticated holiday playground.

If it weren't for the steep cliffs that plunge down to the sea between Nice and Menton it would be easy to forget that 80 per cent of the Alpes-Maritimes is composed of mountains. This is a region of wild, unexplored landscapes, whose slumbering villages – Biot, Saorge, St-Paul-de-Vence – offer visitors a chance to sample the true *douceur de vivre* of rural Provence.

NICE

Nice is capital of the Alpes-Maritimes *département*, the Riviera's largest and most interesting city and France's largest tourist resort. Yet despite its status it remains friendly, full of Mediterranean charm, with its own dialect *(lenga nissarda)* and delicious cuisine.

Nice was originally founded by the Greeks in the 4th century BC. Then the Romans had a settlement at Cimiez, later ruined by Saracens. Nice began to thrive again in the Middle Ages, first under the counts of Provence, then under the Italian dukes of Savoy. Only unified with France in 1860, it retains a strong Italianate character, combining Italian temperament and lifestyle with French finesse and *savoir faire*.

Thanks mainly to the British, by the 1860s Nice was already Europe's most fashionable winter retreat, and exuberant belle-epoque hotels sprang up along the fashionable palm-lined waterfront, aptly named the promenade des Anglais. Nearby, the alleyways and markets of the *vieille ville* contrast boldly with the broad boulevards and designer shops of the modern city. The entire city is cradled by the vineclad foothills of the maritime Alps. This delightful setting has attracted many artists over the years. As a result, Nice is blessed with more museums and galleries than any French town outside Paris.

www.nicetourisme.com

 22H

5 promenade des Anglais ☎ 08 92 70 74 07

Cathédrale Orthodoxe Russe St-Nicolas

A pink and grey Russian Orthodox church, crowned by six green onion-shaped cupolas, built by Tzar Nicolas II in 1903 in memory of his son Nicolas, who is buried in the grounds. Brimming with precious icons, frescoes and treasures, the church still conducts regular services in Russian.

www.acor-nice-com

Nice 1b ✉ Avenue Nicolas-II ☎ 04 93 96 88 02 🕐 Mon–Sat 9:15–12, 2–5:30, Sun 2–5:30 🚌 4, 7, 14, 17, 71, 75 💷 Inexpensive

Cimiez

Nice's smartest residential area owes much of its original cachet to Queen

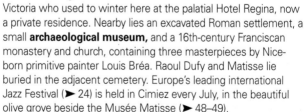

Victoria who used to winter here at the palatial Hotel Regina, now a private residence. Nearby lies an excavated Roman settlement, a small **archaeological museum,** and a 16th-century Franciscan monastery and church, containing three masterpieces by Nice-born primitive painter Louis Bréa. Raoul Dufy and Matisse lie buried in the adjacent cemetery. Europe's leading international Jazz Festival (➤ 24) is held in Cimiez every July, in the beautiful olive grove beside the Musée Matisse (➤ 48–49).

Nice 4a (off map)

Musée Archéologique de Cimiez

✉ 160 avenue des Arènes ☎ 04 93 81 59 57; www.musee-archaologique-nice.org 🕐 Wed–Mon 10–6 🚌 15, 22, 25 💷 Moderate ❓ Guided tours

Musée d'Art Moderne et d'Art Contemporain (MAMAC)

The museum's collections trace the history of French and American avant-garde art from the 1960s to the present: new realists, American pop art, minimalism and the Nice School, in particular its founder Yves Klein. The building, itself a "museum-monument", is a masterpiece of modern architecture with fine views from its rooftop terraces.

www.mamac-nice.org

⊞ Nice 4b ✉ Promenade des Arts ☎ 04 97 13 42 01 ⊘ Tue–Sun 10–6
🚌 3, 4, 5, 6, 7, 9, 10, 14, 17, 25, 30 🍴 Cafe ♿ Free ❓ Gift shop

Musée Masséna

Thanks to a meticulous five-year renovation and a grand reopening in 2008, Nice's superb history museum is back in business. This seaside mansion illustrates the city's modern history by way of portraits of local movers and shakers, glamorous costumes from the belle-epoque period and menus from the roaring 1920s. The flower-filled gardens offer a cool respite from the city bustle.

⊞ Nice 2d ✉ 64 rue de France ☎ 04 93 91 19 10 ⊘ Wed–Mon 10–6
🚌 9, 11, 52, 59, 60, 62 ♿ Free

Musée Matisse

Best places to see, ➤ 48–49.

Musée National Message Biblique Marc Chagall

Located in the heart of a Mediterranean garden, this striking museum was opened by Chagall himself and was specially built to house his "Biblical Message" – a series of 17 monumental canvases evoking the Garden of Eden, Moses and other Old Testament themes. Chagall also made the mosaic and the beautiful blue stained-glass windows in the concert hall.

Other creations, including paintings and sculptures, were donated to the museum after Chagall's death in 1985, making this the most important permanent collection of his work.
www.musee-chagall.fr

🚩 *Nice 3a* ✉ Avenue Docteur-Ménard ☎ 04 93 53 87 20 🕐 Wed–Mon 10–5 🍴 Cafe Apr–Oct 🚌 15, 22 ✋ Expensive ❓ Guided tours

Promenade des Anglais

As its name suggests, this palm-lined promenade, which graciously sweeps round the Baie des Anges (Bay of Angels), was constructed at the expense of Nice's wealthy English residents in the mid-19th century so they could stroll along the shoreline. Today the white wedding-cake style architecture of the luxury belle-epoque hotels are juxtaposed with concrete apartment blocks.

🚩 *Nice 1–2d*

Vieille Ville and cours Saleya

Nice's *vieille ville* (old town) is a maze of dark narrow streets, festooned with flowers and laundry and brimming with cafes, hidden squares and bustling markets. This is the most authentic part of Nice, especially around the cours Saleya, one of France's best fruit and vegetable markets. By night, cafes and restaurants fill the square, making it one of Nice's most animated night spots.

🚩 *Nice 4d* 🚌 All buses ❓ Cours Saleya fruit and vegetable market Tue–Sun am; flower market (all day except Sun pm); flea market Mon

 a walk around Nice Vieille Ville

Start at the western end of cours Saleya.

This square is where Nice's famous outdoor flower, fruit and vegetable market is held (▶ 65), an ideal place to hear the local patois and to taste *socca*, *pissaladière* and other local delicacies (▶ 13).

Head east past the palace of the former dukes of Savoy and the Italianate 18th-century Chapelle de la Misericorde to the yellow house at the end of the square, where Matisse once lived. Turn left into rue Gilly then continue along rue Droite.

Rue Droite contains some of the old town's top galleries and Provence's best bread shops. Palais Lascaris, an ornate 17th-century Genoese-style mansion, houses the Musée des Arts-et-Traditions-Populaires, containing sumptuous period paintings, furnishings and *trompe l'oeil* ceilings.

Continue past Palais Lascaris, until place St-François and the early morning fish market.

Unusally, this is an inland fish market but, before the Paillon river was filled in, fishermen used to land here to sell their catch.

Make an about turn and walk down rue St-Francois. Bear right into rue du Collet, left at place Centrale along rue Centrale, then right into rue Mascoïnat until you reach place Rossetti.

Place Rossetti is dominated by the beautiful baroque Cathédrale Ste-Réparate, with its emerald dome of

Niçoise tiles. Enjoy a coffee in one of the cafes here or try one of the fantastic ice-cream flavours displayed at Fenocchio (➤ 180).

Leave the square along rue Ste-Reparate. At the end, turn right into rue de la Prefecture.

The great violinist Niccolò Paganini lived and died at No 23.

Take a right turn opposite Paganini's house into rue St-Gaètan, which will take you back to cours Saleya.

Distance 2km (1 mile)
Time 1–2 hours, depending on shopping, museum and church visits
Start/end point Cours Saleya ✚ *Nice 4d*
🚌 All buses
Lunch La Cambuse (€€)
✉ 5 cour Saleya
☎ 04 93 80 82 40

The Alpes-Maritimes

ANTIBES

Antibes was founded in the 5th century BC as a Greek trading post, and centuries later was controlled by the dukes of Savoy until the 18th century. Napoléon was held prisoner here in 1794 in Vauban's mighty 17th-century Fort Carré on the eastern edge of town. Today, its massive ramparts protect Old Antibes from flooding. The 16th-century seafront château today houses one of France's best Picasso collections in the **Musée Picasso.**

Old Antibes, hidden behind the ramparts, is a maze of cobbled, winding lanes overflowing with shops, restaurants and bars. Don't miss the bustling morning market in cours Masséna. On the waterfront, Port Vauban, Europe's largest pleasure harbour, hosts some of the most luxurious yachts.

www.antibes-juanlespins.com

✚ 22J

ℹ️ 11 place du Général-de-Gaulle, Antibes ☎ 04 97 23 11 11

Musée Picasso

Best places to see, ➤ 50–51.

BIOT

The charming hilltop village of Biot is a mass of steep cobbled lanes lined with sand-coloured houses capped by orange-tiled roofs, leading up to the arcaded main square. The streets are decorated with huge earthenware jars ablaze with geraniums and tropical plants, as, for centuries, Biot has been a thriving pottery centre. It is also known for its gold and silverwork, ceramics, olive-wood carving and glassworks. Visitors can watch glass-blowers at the Verrerie de Biot demonstrating their distinctive *verre bullé* (bubble glass). Near by is the **Musée Fernand-Léger,** founded in 1959 in memory of cubist painter Fernand Léger who lived at Biot for a

short time and inspired the growth of the craft workshops. The museum contains nearly 400 of his works.
www.biot.fr

✚ 22J

ℹ️ 46 rue St-Sébastien, Biot ☎ 04 93 65 78 00

Musée Fernand-Léger

✉️ Chemin du Vai de Pome ☎ 04 92 91 50 30; www.musee-fernandleger.fr

🕐 Wed–Mon 10–6 🍴 Cafe 👋 Moderate ❓ Call ahead for guided tours

CAGNES-SUR-MER

Cagnes is divided into three: the old fishing quarter and main beach area of Cros-de-Cagnes; Cagnes-Ville, the commercial centre with its smart racecourse beside the sea; and Haut-de-Cagnes. The latter is an inviting hilltop village with brightly coloured houses, crowned by a 14th-century château built by Admiral Rainer Grimaldi as a pirate lookout. Renoir spent the last 11 years of his life nearby at Domaine des Collettes, now the **Musée Renoir**.
www.cagnes-tourisme.com

✚ 22H

ℹ️ 6 boulevard Maréchal-Juin, Cagnes-sur-Mer ☎ 04 93 20 61 64

Musée Renoir

✉️ 19 chemin des collettes, Cagnes-sur-Mer ☎ 04 93 20 61 07

🕐 Wed–Mon 10–12, 2–5 (until 6 Jun–Aug) 👋 Moderate

CANNES

Think Cannes, think movies and film stars, the world-famous film festival (➤ 24), expensive boutiques, palatial hotels and paparazzi!

With so much glitz it is easy to forget that Cannes was a mere fishing village until 1834, when retired British chancellor Lord Brougham, en route to Nice, was enchanted by its warm climate and quaint setting and built a villa here to spend the winter months. Soon hundreds of other aristocrats and royals followed his example. Before long hotels began to spring up along the waterfront. However, it was not until the 1930s that Cannes became a summer resort, made fashionable by visiting Americans. By the 1950s mass summer tourism had taken off and has been the lifeblood of Cannes ever since.

The town is divided into two parts. The Vieux Port and old Roman town of Canois Castrum (now known as le Suquet) occupy a small hill to the west, crowned by an 11th-century castle and watchtower. To the east, modern Cannes is built round la Croisette, one of Europe's most chic promenades, flanked by the sparkling Golfe de la Napoule with its golden beaches of imported sand.

www.cannes.fr

✚ 21J ❓ International Film Festival in May (➤ 24)

🛈 Palais des Festivals, Esplanade Georges Pompidou, 1a Croissette, Cannes

☎ 04 92 99 84 22

CAP-FERRAT

The "Peninsula of Billionaires", with its huge villas hidden in subtropical gardens, has long been a favourite haunt of the rich and famous. A coastal path from Villefranche around the cape past countless tiny azure inlets makes a pleasant stroll.

Cap-Ferrat's finest villa – which would undoubtedly be one of the world's most expensive if it ever came on the market – is the **Villa Ephrussi de Rothschild,** a rose-pink belle-epoque palace constructed by the flamboyant Baroness Béatrice Ephrussi de Rothschild (1864–1934), set in immaculate formal gardens with wonderful sea views. The remarkable interior is lavishly decorated with rare furniture (including some pieces that once belonged to Marie Antoinette), set off by rich carpets, tapestries and an eclectic collection of rare objets d'art.

www.saintjeancapferrat.fr

✚ 23H

🛈 59 avenue Denis Semeria ☎ 04 93 76 08 90

Villa Ephrussi de Rothschild

✉ Chemin du Musée, St-Jean-Cap-Ferrat ☎ 04 93 01 33 09 🕐 Mid-Feb to Oct daily 10–6 (until 7 Jul, Aug); Nov to mid-Feb Sat, Sun 10–6, Mon–Fri 2–6. 🍴 Salon de thé (€€) 💳 Expensive ❓ Guided tours available; gift shop

THE CORNICHES

Three famous corniches (cliff roads) traverse the most scenic and most mountainous stretch of the Côte d'Azur from Nice to Menton via Monaco. Called La Grande (D2564), La Moyenne (N7) and L'Inférieure Corniche, the roads each zig-zag their way along vertiginous ledges at three different elevations. La Grande Corniche, at the highest level, was first constructed by Napoléon and is the best choice for picnickers and lovers of nature.

The steep Corniche Moyenne in the middle is undoubtedly the most dramatic – a cliff-hanging route with hair-raising bends, sudden tunnels and astounding views.

✚ 23H ❓ Avoid L'Inférieure Corniche (N98) in summer, due to heavy traffic

ÈZE

The most strikingly placed and best-preserved Provençal hilltop village, Èze stands high on a rocky pinnacle with amazing views over the Riviera as far as Corsica.

Tall, golden stone houses and a labyrinth of tiny vaulted passages and stairways climb steeply up to the ruins of the Saracen fortress 429m (1,407ft) above sea level, surrounded by an **exotic garden,** bristling with magnificent cacti, succulents and rare palms. Explore the countless craft shops housed in small caves within the rock. At the foot of the hill, the two perfume factories of Galimard and Fragonard both contain fascinating museums.

www.eze-riviera.com

✚ 23H

🛈 Place de Gaulle, Èze ☎ 04 93 41 26 00

Jardin Exotique

✉ Rue du Château ☎ 04 93 41 10 30 🕐 Daily 9–dusk ✋ Moderate

GRASSE

For 400 years Grasse has been the capital of the perfume industry. Until recently 85 per cent of the world's flower essence was created here, and this sleepy, fragrance-filled town is still France's leading centre for the cut-flower market. Learn about the history and alchemy of the perfume industry at the **Musée International de la Parfumerie,**

which reopened after an extensive renovation in 2008. Or take a tour around **Maison Fragonard,** Grasse's largest perfume factory.
www.grasse.fr

✚ 21H

ℹ 3 place de la Foux, Grasse ☎ 04 93 36 21 68

Musée International de la Parfumerie

✉ 2 boulevard du Jeu de Ballon ☎ 04 97 05 58 00;
www.museesdegrasse.com 🕓 Jun–Sep daily 10–7 (Thu until 9); Oct–May Wed–Mon 11–6 💷 Inexpensive

Maison Fragonard

✉ 20 boulevard Fragonard, Grasse ☎ 04 93 36 44 65; www.fragonard.com
🕓 Daily 9–6 💷 Free

MENTON

France's most Italianate resort, with its steep jumble of tall houses, is wedged between a sweeping palm-lined bay and a dramatic mountain backdrop. Menton is France's warmest town, boasting an annual 300 days of sun and resulting in a town bursting with semi-tropical gardens. Menton is also the "lemon capital of the world", smothered in citrus groves. Every February a Lemon Festival (➤ 24), culminating in a procession of floats decorated with citrus fruit, takes place.

The old medieval town has two magnificent churches – Église St- Michel and the Chapelle de la Conception. Also notable are the Musée Jean Cocteau, the Musée de la Préhistoire Régional, boasting the remains of "Menton Man" (30,000BC), and Palais Carnolès, now Menton's main art museum.
www.tourisme-menton.fr

✚ 24H

ℹ Palais de l'Europe, avenue Boyer, Menton ☎ 04 92 41 76 76

MONACO

After the Vatican, Monaco is the world's smallest sovereign state, a 195ha (495-acre) spotlessly clean strip of skyscraper-covered land squeezed between sea and mountains. There are no taxes; attracting the world's highest incomes and the rich and famous.

Monaco is the name of the principality and also the district on the peninsula to the south, containing the old town, a startling contrast to the newer high-rise district of Monte-Carlo, centred round its glitzy casino and designer shops. With so much evident wealth and glamour it is hard to imagine Monaco's turbulent past, at various times occupied by the French, the Spanish and the dukes of Savoy. The present ruling king is Prince Albert II, whose family (the Grimaldis) has ruled Monaco for over 700 years, making it the world's oldest reigning monarchy.

The Grimaldis once held sway over an area that extended along the coast, including Menton and Roquebrune. However, their high taxes provoked a revolt and the principality shrank to its present size. Facing a financial crisis, Charles III of Monaco decided to turn to gambling for his revenue by opening a casino. Such was its success that taxes were soon abolished altogether.

www.visitmonaco.com

✚ 23H

🛈 2a boulevard des Moulins, Monte-Carlo ☎ 0377 92 16 61 16

Casino

Even if you're not a gambler, visit the world's most famous casino, designed in 1878 by Charles Garnier, architect of the Paris Opéra, to see its opulent belle-epoque interior and highly ornate opera house, which has been graced by many of the world's most distinguished opera singers. The dazzlingly place du Casino by night is a must see.

www.casinomontecarlo.com

✉ Place du Casino, Monte-Carlo ☎ 0377 92 06 21 21 🕔 Salons Américans 5pm (2pm Mon–Fri); Salons Européens from 2pm 🚌 1, 4, 6 💷 Salons Américans: free; Salons Européens: expensive ❓ Over 18s; passport required

Cathédrale

Built in 1875 (funded by casino profits), this ostentatious neo-Romanesque cathedral stands on the site of a 13th-century church dedicated to St Nicolas. Among its treasures are two 16th-century retables by Niçois artist Louis Bréa and tombs of the former princes of Monaco and the much-mourned Princess Grace.

✉ 4 rue Colonel-Bellando-de-Castro, Monaco-Ville ☎ 0377 93 30 87 70 🕔 Daily 7–7 🚌 1, 2 💷 Free

Musée Océanographique

Founded by Prince Albert I in 1910 to house his collections of marine flora, fauna, nautical instruments and a 20m (65ft) whale skeleton. The aquarium and museum of marine science is where marine explorer Jacques Cousteau set up his research centre.
www.oceano.mc

✉ Avenue St-Martin, Monaco-Ville ☎ 0377 93 15 36 00 🕐 Oct–Mar daily 10–6; Apr, May, Jun and Sep daily 9:30–7; Jul, Aug daily 9:30–7:30
🍴 Restaurant and bar (€–€€) 🚌 1, 2 ✋ Expensive

Palais du Prince

In summer, when Prince Albert is away, guided tours take visitors through the priceless treasures of the State Apartments and the small Musée Napoléon in the south wing of the palace. The Changing of the Guard ceremony takes place daily at 11:55am.
www.palais.mc

✉ Place du Palais, Monaco-Ville ☎ 0377 93 25 18 31 🕐 Apr, Oct 10:30–5:30; May–Sep 9:30–6:30 🚌 1, 2 ✋ Expensive

MOUGINS

Inside its medieval walls lies one of the Riviera's smartest villages. Photos by Picasso, a past resident, are on display in the **Musée de**

la Photographie. The main attraction is the volume of top restaurants. For a special treat, head to Le Moulin de Mougins (► 180) just outside the village, where celebrity chef Alain Ducasse once learnt his trade.

✚ 21J
ℹ 15 avenue Jean-Charles-Mallet, Mougins
☎ 04 93 75 87 67

Musée de la Photographie

✉ Porte Sarrazine ☎ 04 93 75 85 67 🕐 Jul–Aug daily 10–8; Sep–Oct, Dec–Jun Mon–Fri 10–6, Sat–Sun 11–6 ✋ Free

SAORGE

As you climb the Roya valley into the mountains from the coast, the medieval village of Saorge is a magnificent sight. Hanging 200m (656ft) above the river, its rows of Italian slate-roofed, ochre and blue houses rise in tiers, in the typical style of a *village empilé* (stacked village). Once a Piedmontese border stronghold, Saorge was taken by the French in 1794 but has still retained its unique customs and dialect. Outside the village, the baroque **Franciscan monastery** offers precipitous views down into the valley.

www.saorge.fr

✚ 23G (off map)

ℹ La Mairie, Saorge ☎ 04 93 04 51 23

Couvent des Franciscains

☎ 04 93 04 55 55 🕓 May–Sep 10–12, 2–6; Feb–Apr, Oct 10–12, 2–5

✋ Moderate

ST-PAUL-DE-VENCE

Gently draped over a hill, this picture-postcard hilltop
village was appointed a "Royal Town" in the 16th
century by King François. In the 1920s a group of
young artists including Signac and Bonnard discovered
St-Paul, trading their canvases for accommodation at
la Colombe d'Or (➤ 178). Chagall also lived here and is buried in a
small cemetery just outside the village walls. Today the village is a
tourist honeypot, with coachloads flocking to the nearby
Fondation Maeght and the village's smart shops and galleries. At
night the narrow alleys are enchanting when lit with tiny lanterns.
www.saint-pauldevence.com

✚ 22H

ℹ 2 rue Grande, St-Paul-de-Vence ☎ 04 93 32 86 95

Fondation Maeght

Best places to see, ➤ 40–41.

VENCE

Vence began life as the Roman forum of Vintium. In the Middle Ages it became a bishopric, and its 10th-century cathedral is rich in treasures, including Roman tombstones embedded in the walls and a Chagall mosaic. Henri Matisse moved to Vence in 1941 to escape Allied bombing on the coast, but he then fell seriously ill. Dominican sisters nursed him back to health and, as a gift, he built and decorated the **Chapelle du Rosaire** for them. The chapel's interior is compelling, with Stations of the Cross presented in powerful black line drawings. Matisse worked on this masterpiece well into his 80s, considering it his "ultimate goal, the culmination of an intense, sincere and difficult endeavour".

www.ville-vence.fr

✚ 22H

🛈 Place du Grand-Jardin, Vence ☎ 04 93 58 06 38

Chapelle du Rosaire

✉ 466 avenue Henri-Matisse ☎ 04 93 58 03 26 🕓 Mon, Wed, Fri, Sat 2–5:30, Tue, Thu 10–11:30, 2–5:30 ✋ Inexpensive

VILLEFRANCHE-SUR-MER

Villefranche has changed little since it was founded in the 14th century as a customs-free port (hence its name). Its natural harbour is fringed with red and orange Italianate houses, bars, cafes and restaurants. Steep steps and vaulted passageways climb from the harbour through the *vieille ville*, to the 16th-century citadel, with paintings and sculptures by local artists, including Picasso and Miró. The 14th-century **Chapelle St-Pierre** was decorated in 1957 with frescoes by Villefranche's most famous resident, Jean Cocteau.

www.villefranche-sur-mer.com

✚ 23H

🛈 Jardin François-Binon, Villefranche-sur-Mer ☎ 04 93 01 73 68

Chapelle St-Pierre

✉ Quai Courbet ☎ 04 93 76 90 70 🕓 Apr–Sep daily 10–12, 3–7; Oct, mid-Dec to Mar 10–12, 2–6 ✋ Inexpensive

HOTELS

CANNES
Martinez (€€€€)

This deluxe hotel contains Cannes' top restaurant, La Palme d'Or –
excellent for star spotting during the Film Festival.

✉ 73 boulevard de la Croisette ☎ 04 92 98 73 00; www.hotel-martinez.com

CAP-D'ANTIBES
Bastide du Bosquet (€€–€€€)

Impossibly romantic four-roomed B&B with its own lush garden
set in a millionaire's paradise.

✉ 14 chemin des Sables ☎ 04 93 67 32 29; www.lebosquet06.com
🕐 Closed mid-Nov to mid-Dec

MONACO
Hôtel de Paris (€€€€)

Monte-Carlo's most prestigious address and home of three
excellent restaurants.

✉ Place du Casino ☎ 0377 92 16 30 00; www.hoteldeparismontecarlo.com

NICE
Hôtel Hi (€€)

Quirky modern hotel with funky furnishings, an 24-hour organic
canteen, a hammam and a newly inaugurated private beach.

✉ 3 avenue des Fleurs ☎ 04 97 07 26 26; www.hi-hotel.net

Solara (€–€€)

Excellent value room, some with balconies, in Nice's chic
pedestrian zone.

✉ 7 rue de France ☎ 04 93 88 09 96; www.hotelsolara.com

ST-PAUL-DE-VENCE
La Colomb d'Or (€€€)

Once a modest 1920s cafe where Braque, Matisse, Picasso and
Léger paid for their drinks with canvases. Now a deluxe hotel.

✉ Place du Général-de-Gaulle ☎ 04 93 32 80 02; www.la-colombe-dor.com
🕐 Closed Nov, Dec

VILLEFRANCHE-SUR-MER
Villa Vauban (€€–€€€)

Tranquil and charming nine-bedroom hotel with heaps of period features. Sea views from some rooms, garden patios for others.

✉ 11 avenue General de Gaulle ☎ 04 93 55 94 51; hotelvillavauban.com

RESTAURANTS

ANTIBES
Le Bacon (€€€)

An award-winning fish restaurant midway along the Cap d'Antibes, with six decades of experience.

✉ Boulevard Bacon, Cap-d'Antibes ☎ 04 93 61 50 02; www.restaurantlebacon.com 🕒 Mar–Oct Wed–Sun 12–2, 7:30–10, Tue 7:30–10

BIOT
Auberge du Jarrier (€€)

Imaginative local cuisine and an unmistakable Provençal flavour in an old jar factory.

✉ 30 passage de la Bourgade ☎ 04 93 65 11 68 🕒 Wed–Sun 12–2, 7–9:30

CANNES
La Palme d'Or (€€€)

Master chef Christian Sinicropi stars at what is Cannes' most prestigious restaurant, which boasts two Michelin stars. Also recommended is Le Relais, the Martinez's less expensive poolside eatery.

✉ Hotel Martinez ☎ 04 92 98 74 14; www.hotel-martinez.com 🕒 Wed–Sat 12:30–2, 8–10

ÈZE
La Chèvre d'Or (€€€)

Breathtaking sea views and inspired French cuisine at one of the Rivera's finest restaurants.

✉ 3 rue du Barri ☎ 04 92 10 66 60; www.chevredor.com
🕒 Mid-Mar to Oct lunch Fri–Sun, dinner daily

MONACO
La Salière (€€–€€€)
An Italian restaurant favoured by the stars, and worth every penny. Try crisp *frutti di mare* and searing hot pizza.

✉ 14 quai Jean-Charles-Rey ☎ 0377 92 05 25 82 🕙 Daily 12–2, 7:30–10

MOUGINS
Le Moulin de Mougins (€€€)
A bastion of Provençal cuisine, headed by celebrated chef Sébastien Chambru. Less expensive lunchtime set menus available.

✉ Notre-Dame de Vie ☎ 04 93 75 78 24; www.moulindemougins.com
🕙 Wed–Sun 12–8, 8–10

NICE
Chantecler (€€€)
Nice's leading restaurant and a bastion of French gastronomy.

✉ Hôtel Negresco, 37 promenade des Anglais ☎ 04 93 16 64 00
🕙 Wed–Sun 12:30–2, 7:30–10

Fenocchio (€)
The best ice creams on the Côte d'Azur, bar none.

✉ 2 Place Rossetti ☎ 04 93 80 72 52 🕙 Daily 9am–midnight

La Mérenda (€€)
This tiny restaurant has an irresistible menu of Niçois specialities, prepared by one of France's outstanding chefs – Dominic Le Stanc.

✉ 4 rue de la Terrace ☎ No telephone 🕙 Mon–Fri 12–2, 7–9 ❓ No credit cards accepted

VENCE
La Lilote (€€)
Romantically placed on a tranquil square, inventive dishes include medallions of lamb in a white truffle sauce, and teppenyaki scallops with chervil.

✉ 5 rue de l'Evêché ☎ 04 93 24 27 82; www.lalitote.com 🕙 Tue–Sat 12:30–2, 7–10, Sun 12:30–2

SHOPPING

FOOD AND DRINK
Alziari
This old family shop presses their own olive oil and sells *olives de Nice* by the kilo. A veritable Niçois institution.
✉ 14 rue Saint-François-de-Paule, Nice ☎ 04 93 85 76 92 🕐 Tue–Sat 8:30–12, 2–6

Cave de la Tour
Superb wine shop in Nice old town, with cheap daily lunch and tasting room to the rear.
✉ 3 Rue de la Tour, Nice ☎ 04 93 80 03 31 🕐 Tue–Sun 10–7

Confiserie Florian
Purchase crystalized pears, cactus leaves and other edible fruit from this working sweet factory, or take the interactive tour.
✉ 14 quai Papacino, Nice ☎ 04 93 55 43 50; www.confiserieflorian.com
🕐 Daily 9–12, 2–6:30

SPECIALIST SHOPS
L'Atelier des Jouets
A magical shop full of sturdy, educational toys and games in wood, metal and cloth. Ideal children's gifts.
✉ 1 place de l'Ancien-Sénat, Nice ☎ 04 93 13 09 60 🕐 Daily 10:30–7. Closed Wed am

Cannes English Bookshop
Thousands of novels and cookbooks, from classic writers to local expat authors.
✉ 11 rue Bivouac Napoléon, Cannes ☎ 04 93 99 40 08 🕐 Mon–Sat 10–6:45

ENTERTAINMENT

NIGHTLIFE
Blast
Currently the cours Saleya's hottest spot with open-air cocktail bar and big sofas to lounge in.
✉ Place Charles Felix, Nice ☎ 04 93 80 00 50 🕐 Daily 6pm–2am

Café de Paris

Celebrated cafe and brasserie by day, sip cocktails on the terrace or head through to the *bar des jeux* gaming room in the evening.

✉ Place du Casino, Monaco ☎ 0377 92 16 20 20 🕐 Daily 10am–4am

Ghost Bar

Rocking cocktail bar with friendly crowd and busy dancefloor.

✉ 3 rue de la Barillerie, Nice ☎ 04 93 92 93 37 🕐 Daily 10pm–3am

Le Guest

Popular Niçois nightspot on the old port, with modernist decor.

✉ 5 quai des Deux-Emmanuel, Nice ☎ 04 93 56 83 83 🕐 Daily 11:30pm–5am

Mocca

Low key in the evening with zany cocktails and nibbles, becomes a raucous dance-fest until late.

✉ 1 Boulevard de la Croisette, Cannes ☎ 04 93 68 93 00 🕐 Daily 6pm–2am

La Siesta

One of the Côte d'Azur's most exotic nightclubs with open-air dance floors, fountains, flaming torches and a wave-shaped casino.

✉ Route du Bord-de-la-Mer (between Antibes and la Brague) ☎ 04 93 33 31 31 🕐 Mid-May to mid-Sep daily midnight–4am (winter Thu–Sat only)

CLASSICAL ENTERTAINMENT

Cinéma Mercury

Huge programme of art-house and vintage films all shown in their original language.

✉ 16 place Garibaldi, Nice ☎ 04 93 55 37 81 🕐 Daily 5–11

Monaco Openair Cinema

English-language blockbusters shown alfresco all summer. Like a drive-in movie without the hassle.

✉ Parking du Chemin Des Pecheurs, Monaco ☎ 08 92 68 00 72; www.cinemasporting.com

Opéra de Nice

Home of the Nice Opera, the Philharmonic Orchestra and Ballet Corps, a rococo extravaganza in red and gold modelled on the Naples opera house.

✉ 4/6 rue St-François-de-Paule, Nice ☎ 04 92 17 40 00; www.opera-nice.org 🚌 All buses

Théâtre Nacional de Nice (TTN)

This modern theatre presents world-class shows.

✉ Promenade des Arts, Nice ☎ 04 93 13 90 90; www.tnn.fr
🚌 All buses

SPORTS

Guigo Marine

Tired of lazing on the beach? Book a deep-sea fishing trip.

✉ 9 avenue 11-Novembre, Antibes ☎ 04 93 34 17 17;
www.guigomarine.com 🕐 Jun–Oct

Isola 2000

Day trips from Nice coach station include a ski pass.

☎ 04 93 23 15 15; www.isola2000.com

Monaco Formula 1 Racing

Call up and have a Ferrari delivered to any location in Monaco. Price is €50 for a Grand Prix circuit, €100 if you want to drive yourself.

☎ 06 28 34 62 15; www.f1monaco-racing.com

Moorings

Small yachts for hire in Nice port, with or without crew.

✉ Quai Papacino, Nice ☎ 0800 80 30 30; www.moorings.fr

Roller Station

Rent a skateboard, scooter or rollerblades and zip down the Promenade.

✉ 49 quai des Etats Unis, Nice ☎ 04 93 62 99 05; www.roller-station.com
🕐 Daily Apr–Sep 9:30–8; Oct–Mar 10–6:30

Index

Acknowledgements

The Automobile Association wishes to thank the following photographers, companies and picture libraries for their assistance in the preparation of this book.

Abbreviations for the picture credits are as follows – (t) top; (b) bottom; (l) left; (r) right; (c) centre; (AA) AA World Travel Library

4l Aups, AA/A Baker; **4c** Monaco, AA/A Baker; **4r** Gordes, AA/A Baker; **5l** Pernes le Fountaines, AA/C Sawyer; **5c** Vaison Le Romaine, AA/R Strange; **6/7** Aups, AA/A Baker; **8/9** Flower Parade, Nice, AA/N Ray; **10/11t** Cours Saleya, Nice, AA/C Sawyer; **10c** Fisherman, Bandol, AA/R Strange; **10bl** Eze, AA/A Baker; **10br** Gordes, AA/C Sawyer; **11c** Church of St-Sauveur, Sorge, AA/R Moore; **11b** Grand Canyon du Verdon, AA/C Sawyer; **12/13t** La Tarte Tropezienne, St-Tropez, AA/C Sawyer; **12/13b** Aix en Provence, AA/R Strange; **12** Miel de Provence, Digne les Bains, AA/C Sawyer; **13c** Cours Massena, Antibes, AA/C Sawyer; **13b** Fish, Marseille, AA/B Smith; **14l** Olives for sale, Nyon, AA/C Sawyer; **14c** Sweets, Apt, AA/C Sawyer; **14/15** Honey, Menton, AA/A Baker; **15t** Ricard Pastis, AA/R Strange; **15c** Pastis, Menton, AA/A Baker; **15b** Champagne, AA/B Rieger; **16/17** Beach, Nice, AA/C Sawyer; **16b** Camargue, horses, AA/C Sawyer; **17t** Wine, Chateauneuf de Pape, AA/C Sawyer; **17c** Allee des Stars, Cannes, AA/C Sawyer; **17b** Boules, St Tropez, AA/C Sawyer; **18/19** Cours Massena, Antibes, AA/C Sawyer; **18b** Fragonard, perfume, AA/C Sawyer; **19t** Casino of Monte-Carlo, Monaco, AA/A Baker; **19b** Harbour, St-Tropez, AA/C Sawyer; **20/21** Monaco, AA/A Baker; **27** Train, Digne les Baines, AA/C Sawyer; **28** Bus, Provence, AA/C Sawyer; **28/29** Malaucene, AA/A Baker; **32** Policeman, Paris, AA/M Jourdan; **34/35** Gordes, AA/A Baker; **36** Les Calanques, AA/B Smith; **36/37** Les Calanques, AA/C Sawyer; **38** Flamingoes, Camargue, AA/C Sawyer; **38/39** Salin de Giraud, AA/C Sawyer; **39** White Horse, Camargue. AA/C Sawyer; **40/41** Fondation Maecht, AA/C Sawyer; **42/43t** Church, Gordes, AA/C Sawyer; **42/3b** Gordes, © Jon Arnold Images Ltd/Alamy; **44t** Grand Canyon du Verdon, AA/C Saywer; **44b** Lac de St Croix, AA/C Sawyer; **45** Lac de St Croix, AA/C Sawyer; **46/47** Mont St Victoire, AA/C Sawyer; **47** Barrage de Bimont Dam, AA/T Oliver; **48** Matisse Museum, Nice, AA/C Sawyer; **49** Matisse Museum, Nice, AA/C Sawyer; **50/51** Musee Picasso in Antibes, AA/C Sawyer; **52** Roussillion, AA/R Strange; **52/3** Roussillon, AA/C Sawyer; **54** Theatre Antique, Orange, AA/R Strange; **54/55t** Theatre Antique, Orange, AA/A Baker; **54/55b** Theatre Antique, Orange, AA/R Strange; **56/57** Pernes le Fountaines, AA/C Sawyer; **58/59** Mardi Gras, Nice, AA; **60/61** Camargue, horse-riding, AA/C Sawyer; **62/63** Beach, Cannes, AA/C Sawyer; **64/65** Cours Massena, Antibes, AA/C Sawyer; **66/67** Grand Canyon du Verdon, AA/C Sawyer; **68/69** Eze. AA/C Sawyer; **70** Gourdon, AA/A Baker; **72** Suze-la-Rousse, AA/A Baker; **74/75** Vaison Le Romaine, AA/R Strange; **77** Seguret, AA/A Baker; **78** Avignon, AA/A Baker; **78/9** Rue de la Republique, Avignon, AA/Y Levy; **80** Palais des Papes, Avignon, AA/R Strange; **80/81** Palais de Papes, Avignon, AA/R Strange; **82/83** Castle of Avignon, AA/C Sawyer; **83** Pont St Benezet, Avignon, AA/R Strange; 84 Market, AA/C Sawyer; **85** Cavaillon, AA/A Baker; **86c** Chateauneuf du

Pape, AA/C Sawyer; **86b** Vineyard, Chateauneuf du Pape, AA/C Sawyer; **87** Seguret, AA/A Baker; **88** Fontaine-de-Vaucluse, AA/R Strange; **88/89** Apt, AA/C Sawyer; **90** Lourmarin, Le Restaurant du Moulin, AA/C Sawyer; **90/91** Bonnieux, view to Luberon, AA/R Strange; **91** Oppede-le-Vieux, AA/A Baker; **92/93t** Menerbes, AA/R Strange; **92/93** Fontaine de Vaucluse, AA/C Sawyer; **94/5** Roman theatre in Orange, AA/Y Levy; **96/97** Vaison La Romaine, AA/C Sawyer; **96** Vaison La Romaine, AA/C Sawyer; **105** Stes-Maries-de-la-Mer, AA/R Strange; **106** Marseille, AA/C Sawyer; **107c** Basilique Notre-Dame de la Garde, Marsielle, AA/C Sawyer; **107b** La Canebiere, Marseille; **108** Chateau d'If, Marseille, AA/C Sawyer; **108/109** Cours Mirabeau, Aix-en-Provence, AA/C Sawyer; **109** Cezanne Plaque, Aix-en-Provence, AA/R Strange; **110** St Sauveur, Aix-en-Provence, AA/C Sawyer; **111** Cezanne house, Aix-en-Provence; **112/113** Chaine des Alpilles, AA/C Sawyer; **114** Les Alyscamps, Arles, AA/A Baker; **114/115** Eglise St Trophime, Arles, AA/C Sawyer; **115** Arles, AA/A Baker; **116t** Eglise St Trophime, Arles, AA/C Sawyer; **116/117** Espace Van Gogh, Arles, AA/A Baker; **117** Museon Arletan, Arles, AA/A Baker; **118** Hotel Nord-Pinus, Arles, AA/C Sawyer; **119** Museon Arlaten, Arles, AA/A Baker; **120/121** Les Roches Blanches, Cassis, AA/C Sawyer; **121** Ste-Maries-de-la-Mer, AA/R Strange; **122t** Musee des Alpilles, AA/A Baker; **122b** St-Remy-de-Provence, AA/C Sawyer; **122/123** Tarascon, AA/R Strange; **132/133** St-Tropez waterfront, AA/A Baker; **133** La Citadelle, St-Tropez, AA/C Sawyer; **134/135** Eglise St-Tropez, AA/C Sawyer; **134b** Musee de l'Annonciade, St-Tropez, AA/C Sawyer; **135** Boules, Place des Lices, St-Tropez, AA/C Sawyer; **136** Market, AA/Y Levy; **136/137** Harbour, St-Tropez, AA/C Sawyer; **138** Aups, AA/A Baker; **138/139t** Bormes-les-Mimosas, AA/T Oliver; **138/139b** Cogoline, AA/C Sawyer; **140/141** Miramar beach, AA/R Moore; **141** Cathedral, Frejus, AA/C Sawyer; **142** Hyeres, AA/B Smith; **143** Colmars, AA/R Moore; **144** Digne les Bains, Baths, AA/C Sawyer; **144/145** Entrevaux, AA/C Sawyer; **145** Forcalquier, AA/A Baker; **146** Greoux-les-Bains, AA/A Baker; **146/147** Chapelle Notre-Dame de Beauvoir, Moustiers, AA/A Baker; **148/149** Briancon, AA/R Strange; **150** Sisteron, AA/C Sawyer; **159** Villefrance-sur-Mer. AA/R Moore; **160** Colline du Chateau, Nice, AA/C Sawyer; **161** Cathedral Orthodox Russe, Nice, AA/C Sawyer; **162** Museum of Modern Art, AA/C Sawyer; **163** Promenade des Anglais, Nice, AA/C Sawyer; **164/165** Palais Lascaris in Nice, AA/C Sawyer; **166/167** Juan-les-Pins, AA/A Baker; **167** Cagnes-Sur-Mer, AA/R Strange; **168** Versace shop window, AA/A Mockford & N Bonetti; **168/169** Cannes harbour, AA/C Sawyer; **170/171** Eze, AA/A Baker; **170** Fragonard perfume, Grasse, AA/C Sawyer; **171** Menton, AA/C Sawyer; **172/173** Monaco, AA/A Baker; **173** Monte Carlo, Casino, AA/C Sawyer; **174** Le Manior de l'Etana, Mougins, AA/C Sawyer; **174/175** Sorge, AA/R Moore; **176** Vence, AA/R Strange; **176/177** St Paul de Vence, AA/C Sawyer

Every effort has been made to trace the copyright holders, and we apologise in advance for any unintentional omissions or errors. We would be please to apply any corrections in any following edition of this publication.

Sight locator index

This index relates to the maps on the covers. We have given map references to the main sights of interest in the book. Grid references in italics indicate sights featured on town maps. Some sights within towns may not be plotted on the maps.